Marine Shells of the Pacific Northwest

Marguerite Smith-
Huntington Park-
24525- 13th Ave-So
Kent Wash- 98031
Phone- 824-7399-

by

Tom Rice

PHOTOGRAPHED BY A SPECIAL DIRECT
COLOR PROCESS BY ELLIS H. ROBINSON

© 1971 by Ellison Industries, Inc.
Edmonds, Washington 98020

First Printing June, 1971

Any part of this Publication may be reproduced
in any form with permission of the Publisher.

ISBM-0-912-488-04-2

Introduction

Nearly everyone who has strolled along the shore has noticed the bleached, dead remains of shells scattered about where the tide has left them. Possibly you have picked up a few to decorate a garden or fish bowl. Perhaps you have even wondered what made these shells and where it lived and what was its name. Or, maybe you have dug clams on one of the many sand beaches of the Pacific Northwest and are familiar with a few of the larger species of that group. Did you know that within the Pacific Northwest area there are more than nine hundred different species of marine shells?

Of course in this small volume we could not cover all of the species one could find within our area, but we have attempted to illustrate all of the more common, larger species. I have limited myself to species which occur in the area of the coasts of British Columbia, Washington, Oregon and northern California, but many of the species included have a much larger range.

The history of collecting shells in the Pacific Northwest dates back many centuries – the native Indian tribes used one of the local species as money. Scientific collections were started over one hundred years ago by missionaries who sent their specimens to the Smithsonian Institution or England for identification. The growing numbers of people using the beaches of this area, however, have shown a need for a handy, simply worded guide which can be understood by anyone of nearly any age.

With the growing awareness amongst all sectors of the public to their environment, those of us who have been interested in the animal and plant life of the sea and its shore should endeavor to pass along whatever information we can. It is with this in mind that this book was started.

Acknowledgements

There are a number of people to whom I owe thanks for assistance in the preparation of this volume. Dr. James H. McLean of the Los Angeles County Museum of Natural History offered many suggestions as to the proper identification of many of the gastropods illustrated and other helpful suggestions came from Allyn G. Smith of the California Academy of Sciences in San Francisco. My thanks to Colonel George A. Hanselman of San Diego, California for his help with the section concerning chitons. However, any missidentifications or other mistakes and/or omissions are my own.

I would also like to thank the following collectors for loan of specimens used for illustrative purposes: Mrs. Thomas Marshall of Seattle, Mr. and Mrs. Gerald L. Ward of Edmonds, Washington and Mrs. Richard Wingard of Gig Harbor, Washington. Without their help and encouragement this booklet would have been much more difficult to produce. A special thanks to Ellis Robinson of Ellison Industries, Inc. for his understanding and patience and for the opportunity to undertake this project in the first place.

The drawings used in this volume are the work of Mrs. Agnes Ward of Edmonds, Washington.

What Are Shells?

Shells, or more properly mollusks, are generally that group of invertebrate (without backbone) animals which have an external calcareous shell. This group, next in size in the animal kingdom to the insects, includes snails, clams, chitons, octopus, squid, mussels, but not the so-called shellfish such as crabs, shrimp, etc.

Mollusks, as with other animals and plants, are divided into related groups. All mollusks belong to the phylum **Mollusca**, which is then divided into six (or seven depending upon which "expert" one follows) Classes—these are discussed below. The Classes are further divided into Families and these, in turn, are separated into genera. The final division is to species. That is, each genus (the singular of genera) contains numerous species. In the text of this booklet you will note I use the scientific names for the different shells. The first Latin name, the name of the Genus, is capitalized while the second, or species, name is not. The reason Latin is used for scientific names is that it is a "dead" and therefore unchanging language and is used by collectors the world over. Common names (those of general use locally are included in the text) can lead to problems as the same common name is used in different areas to refer to entirely different species of shells. Actually, when learning a new shell name it's just as easy to learn the proper scientific name.

The Six Classes

AMPHINEURA - Chitons

This group consists of mollusks which have eight plates or valves, usually visible on the upper surface of the animal and which are held in place by a "girdle". These animals live attached to rocks or other surfaces. Some deepwater shell-less forms are separated into a second Class (Solenogastres). Chitons are illustrated on Plates 1 through 5.

GASTROPODA – Snails

Possessing a single shell (or in the case of sea slugs or nudibranchs and garden slugs, no shell or only a tiny internal remnant of a shell) in many different shapes. Gastropoda sometimes possess a horny or calcareous plate used to close the aperture or mouth when the snail retracts into the shell, this is known as an operculum. These are illustrated on Plates 6 through 24.

SCAPHOPODA – Tusk Shells

These shells are tube-like, smaller at one end and sometimes curved. This is a small Class represented locally by only a few species. See the *Dentalium* on Plate 24.

PELECYPODA – Clams or Bivalves

With two parts or valves to the complete shell; these are held together by a hinge arrangement and/or ligament. Pelecypoda means "hatchet-foot" and the local species of this Class are illustrated on Plates 26 through 39.

CEPHALOPODA – Octopus, Squid and Cuttlefish

The word Cephalopoda means "head-foot" and these active animals are equipped with numerous tentacles. Locally represented by more than two dozen species, we have not included them in this booklet because, among other reasons, of the difficulty of obtaining specimens.

MONOPLACOPHORA

This rare Class has shells which look like the gastropod limpets, but are an ancient Class long thought extinct for the past 450 million years. Recently living specimens have been dredged in depths over three miles off Costa Rica and other areas. As far as is known no species occur locally.

Collecting Shells

REGULATIONS

The states of Washington, Oregon and California, as well as the province of British Columbia, have certain restrictions as to methods of collecting and limitations as to the size and numbers of certain species of mollusks that you may possess. Please contact the State Fish and Game Commissions or Department of Fisheries in the capitol cities for copies of the regulations—these regulations are usually available in the various tide tables one can obtain at sporting goods stores, fishing resorts, etc.

For those contemplating collecting in the state of Oregon a special word of caution. There are a number of protected beaches on this state's coast where collecting is prohibited and on all beaches there is a strict limit as to number of species of any marine animals you may collect. For specific information contact the Fish Commission of Oregon: 307 State Office Building, Portland, Oregon 97201.

In California there are also prohibitions against collecting on some state-owned beaches. A fishing license is also required for anyone who wishes to collect live specimens—specific prohibitions and regulations can be obtained where the fishing licenses are purchased.

WHERE TO LOOK

The drift line can give you an idea of the shells you might look for on a particular beach and sometimes the drift can yield good "finds" in the presence of deepwater shells which have washed ashore. But usually the best shells, as far as specimens for a collection are concerned, are found alive with the original animal still at "home". Should your "live" shells be running around on six "feet" it's no longer inhabited by its builder, but has been appropriated by a hermit crab as its temporary "mobile" home.

Different species of mollusks have very specialized habitats in which they occur. Some are found only on mud flats of calm bays, others only on the undersides of rocks in areas of heavy surf. Still others, a very few, are adaptable enough to occur in several diverse habitats.

The best area in which to look for shells in order to observe the most species are the intertidal rock areas of both the coastal beach and the inland saltwater areas. As most animals have an intense dislike for the drying effects of the sun they can be found hiding under the rocks—one very important thing to remember, ALWAYS TURN THE ROCKS BACK once you have searched under it for specimens!! Unless this is done the animals and plant life, and there's usually lots of it, on both the upper and lower surfaces, will die as you have blatantly reversed their universe and exposed them to conditions with which they cannot cope. Once a rock has been set upside-down and not returned to its original position, the life on it dies and it may take as long as ten (yes, 10) years for that life to regain a foothold on that rock!

Although most people are content to limit themselves to intertidal collecting you might want to explore other methods of collecting shells. Diving, either free-diving or with SCUBA, dredging, trapping or trawling are all used to obtain shells.

The various habitants of the different groups of shells are discussed in the text.

A Code of Ethics for Shell-Collectors

BECAUSE I appreciate our heritage of wildlife and natural resources, I WILL make every effort to protect and preserve them, not only for my own future enjoyment, but also for the benefit of generations to come.

I WILL make sure that I leave things as I found them during all of my shelling explorations.

I WILL return rocks, boulders, kelp and sea weeds to their original positions after looking beneath them.

I WILL refill the holes I dig and the burrows I uncover.

I WILL take only those specimens that I know I can clean and use.

I WILL leave behind the damaged and young specimens so that they may live and multiply.

I WILL never knowingly deplete an area of an entire species.

I WILL respect the property rights of others; treat public land as I would the property of my friends and collect on private beaches only with the owner's permission.

I WILL leave behind no trash or litter and discard no burning material.

I WILL build fires with care, but only where legal and permissable.

I WILL obey all wildlife laws.

I WILL always use good outdoor manners.

Cleaning Your Shells

REMOVING THE ANIMAL FROM THE SHELL

A problem one encounters immediately in the "shell game" – beginning a collection – is how to properly clean the specimens. This, of course, is no problem if you limit yourself to specimens without the animal or drift material. However, as mentioned, the best specimens are live-collected and thus, unless you wouldn't mind the worst odor you might ever encounter when the animal starts to decay, you'd better decide to remove or preserve the animal. Small specimens, usually all those under one-half-inch, can probably be best preserved by placing the shell, animal and all, into a small container of isopropyl (rubbing) alcohol and leaving it there for a day or two. Remove the specimen from the alcohol and let it dry in a dry shady spot (NEVER dry shells in the sun as it will bleach away the natural colors). Gastropods with operculums are best placed in a container of salt-water until dead (usually overnight) and then preserved in the alcohol, thus keeping the operculum in a visible position; immediately placing the live animal into alcohol causes a sudden contraction and the operculum might be drawn so far back into the shell that it cannot be seen.

Should you pick up specimens with hermit crabs living within—and this sometimes is the only way to find certain small or deeper water species—the removal of the crab might prove a problem. But a simple method is to place the specimen in a container of fresh water overnight and the next day use a gentle tug and the crab should come out quite easily. Or after the night in fresh water, place the specimen in alcohol and upon removal when time permits, the crab can be gently pulled out.

Larger specimens of Pelecypods and Gastropoda are best cleaned by complete removal of the animal. Bivalves (Pelecypoda) can be placed in a pan of cold water, put on the stove and brought to a boil. As soon as you can handle the specimens after removal of the pan from the stove, remove the animals from those specimens which have opened as they die. Carefully pry open the valves of any which failed to open and remove the animal. Be careful not to break the hinge (the part that holds the two valves together) and it's a good idea to fasten the shells together with twine or a rubber band while it dries—or to dry in a flat, butterfly-like position with the valves spread open.

Large Gastropoda are also placed in cold water and brought to a boil. The animal can then be removed by using a bent pin or a needle which has been secured in the end of a small dowel. Carefully exert a slowly increasing amount of pressure, just enough to start the animal spiralling out, too much and you'll likely break off the tail end or liver area. Should this happen and you cannot shake out the broken end you might try one of two methods. Add a few drops of isopropyl alcohol or formalin and let the portion dry and eventually fall out. Or you can place the shell in a container of fresh water and each day take the specimen out and give it a good shaking to dislodge the remaining portion of animal and if unsuccessful renew the water and try again another day. Eventually the stubborn piece will come out.

One important thing to remember when working with gastropods possessing an operculum. Save it! When you remove the snail from its shell the operculum will usually remain attached to the foot, pull it free and dry it next to its shell and when both are thoroughly dry glue the operculum to a bit of cotton and place it in its natural position in the aperture (mouth) of the shell.

Limpets, slipper shells, etc. prove little problem as the animal will either fall out upon boiling or can easily be removed. These groups do not have an operculum.

CLEANING THE SHELL ITSELF

Cleaning the outer surface of a shell presents many varied problems and as many solutions. I shall not go into too much of a discussion on this other than to give a few basic methods. The best all-around cleaner for the attached algae, lime growths, etc. which accumulate on most shells, is a bath in a household bleach such as Chlorox, Purex, etc. Some species should, however, never be treated in this manner—such as the olives, cowries (which do not occur in this area) or other naturally "shiny" species as it will dull the natural lustre of the shell. But most shells will not be harmed by a short bleach bath. Remember, if you want to preserve a specimen with its periostracum (outer "skin") intact DO NOT bathe it in bleach, but as with other fragile shells give it a bath of detergent and water.

The best implement to use along with either the bleach or detergent bath is an old tooth brush. Using this and running tap water you can scrub away any dirt and most attached algae. Barnacles and other animals such as worm shells, which have attached themselves to the shell, can be removed by applying a bit of pressure with a cleaning tool such as those used to remove the animal or old dental tools or something similar. Careful use of these tools will enable you to remove nearly all of the various attached growths without damage to the shell itself.

Some people might recommend use of acid to clean shells—this is the WORST thing you could do! Not only is it hazardous to you, but can easily ruin your specimen. It also gives the shell a very unnatural look. The best advice I can give pertaining to acid is to leave it alone! A shell even with attachments looks better in the collection than one obviously acid cleaned.

To help preserve the natural color of the specimen I recommend applying a light coating of mineral or baby oil. This does not alter the color or the scientific value of the specimen, but will keep it from looking dried-out and keep it more "natural" looking. It will also help preserve the periostracum should you desire.

Chitons present a special problem in both preservation and cleaning. Since the best feature for identification in this group is the girdle you should attempt to preserve this portion. To do this the best method is to tie the animal in a flat position, while alive—either as soon as it is removed from its rock or when you stop collecting—on a wooden board such as a tongue depressor or a glass or plastic slide and placed in a "killing" jar of alcohol (50% isopropyl). After a day in this solution the specimen can be removed from its board and placed in a solution of 50% isopropyl and 50% glycerin (at this time, should you wish, you can carefully cut the animal away from the shell and girdle so that the undersides of the valves can be seen. Use a razor blade or small sharp knife for this operation.). After staying in this solution from several days to two weeks—depending upon the size of the specimen—remove it and retie it to the board and then let the specimen dry thoroughly in a shaded place. When all this has been done you might carefully clean the upper surface of the valves with a needle to rid them of algae, tube worms, barnacles, etc.

Many collectors maintain "wet" chiton collections. In this type of collection the specimen is tied to a plastic or glass slide, placed in the "killing" jar and upon removal placed in a specimen jar or vial of alcohol for display. Other collectors keep several girdle specimens and with the rest of any one species keep only the valves which are reglued in their natural order after removal from the animal. This is done by bringing the animal to a boil as with other shells and removing the valves; to clean these they can be given the bleach bath, tooth brush treatment.

The Collection Itself

Once you have collected and cleaned the shell you might feel that's all there is, but no, there's more. A good, scientifically valuable collection needs another item. That is a label indicating several important pieces of data—the least important of which is the name of the shell! Most important is the place of collection and the habitat in which the animal was found. This, simply put, is the name of the beach and whether the shell was attached, buried in sand, or just where was it found. Additional items are the date on which the shell was collected, just the month and year are ample though some collectors prefer the exact day also. Indicate on the label, as well, the area of the beach on which the shell was collected, i.e. upper area, mid-tide area or low-tide area. Should the specimen come from dredging or trapping the depth and type of bottom should be noted. Any other pieces of interesting data can also be included on this collection label, any remarks you might make concerning the live animal's appearance, if it was feeding, laying eggs, etc. will prove valuable to someone later on.

As to how to house your collection this is a very individual choice. Most anything will do from a show box to a specially constructed shell cabinet. The one important thing to remember in this decision is to protect your specimens from undue exposure to sunlight and to keep them safe from breakage—use cotton or individual plastic boxes or vials. Most of all, have fun and keep your shells where you can enjoy them.

The Text

The text and plates of this book are arranged in a systematic order, i.e. the species illustrated progress from most primitive to most developed within each Class. The Amphineura are followed by the Gastropoda and Scaphopoda and finally the Pelecypoda.

Each species illustrated is indicated by a number, this number also accompanies the text material concerning that species. The text is arranged so that material relating to any species is within a page or two of the illustration.

In the discussion of each species the following information is given: the scientific name (italicized) and the author who first described the species and the year of description; the local common name; the range of the species along the coast; any distinguishing features which might be useful in separating the species from other related forms; and the relative abundance of the species. This latter bit of information is only an indication as to frequency of collection by various collectors and does not indicate the relative abundance of that species in nature, but does indicate that the habitat of that species is either well-known or unknown or inaccessible. I have used five terms to indicate this information as follows: common, not uncommon, uncommon, not common and rare. These are used in a decending order of frequency of collection —i.e. a species labeled "common" can usually be found with little effort, while those labeled "rare" have been seldom collected.

Amphineura

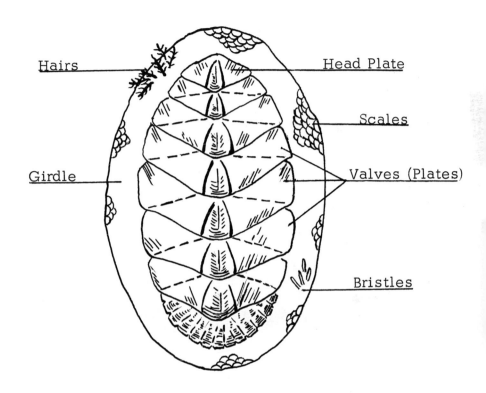

Hairs

Head Plate

Scales

Girdle

Valves (Plates)

Bristles

Chitons, the Class Amphineura, are always found attached to some type of surface with the exception of the Giant chiton (see Plate 5) which can be found crawling along on the reef, amongst rocks on the beach or on sand amongst rocks in the intertidal zone. Most chitons seem to prefer sides or undersides of rocks, though some will live in exposed situations on the tops of rocks or on the reef. Specimens can also be found on pilings and occasionally on dead clam shells.

PLATE 1

152 points   Book 10

1. *Tonicella lineata* Wood, 1815 is the **Red-lined Chiton**, probably one of the most common of this group in our area. Sometimes it appears to be greenish or bluish due to attached minute algae. Found in the intertidal zone from Alaska to central California.

2. *Tonicella insignis* Reeve, 1847. This maroon-red chiton, with the white stripes an identification feature, is not common throughout its range of Alaska to Puget Sound.

3. *Mopalia hindsii* Reeve, 1847 ranges from Alaska to central California and can be distinguished by the fairly numerous short, fine girdle hairs as compared with the next species, to which otherwise it can appear almost identical. Not uncommon in the northern portion of the range.

4. *Mopalia laevior* Pilsbry, 1918 is distinguished from the above by its fewer, longer straggling girdle hairs and the fact that the girdle extends into the space between the valves. Range is from Alaska to central California, not uncommon in northern part.

PLATE 2

5. *Mopalia lignosa* Gould, 1846 is fairly common from Alaska to central California and is distinguished by the finely pustulate sculpture and the girdle which is strewn with simple bristles. The left illustration is the common color; the others rare color forms.

6. *Mopalia muscosa* Gould, 1846 is commonly called the **Mossy Chiton** because with its extremely hairy girdle and its habitat on tops of rocks it can become completely covered with algae. Alaska to northern Baja California, common in most of the area. The blue interior is a constant feature.

Plate 1

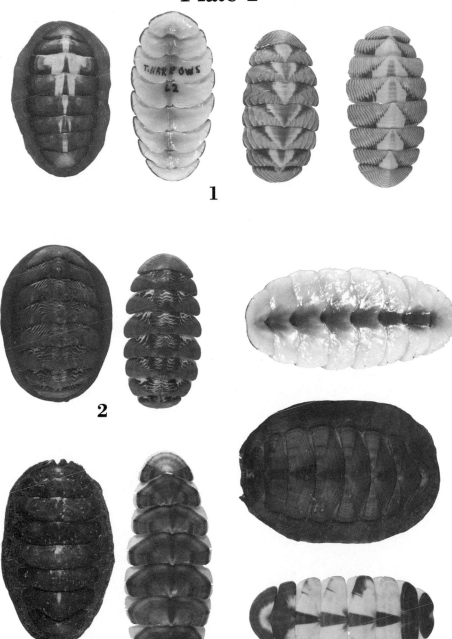

Plate 2

5

6

Plate 3

7

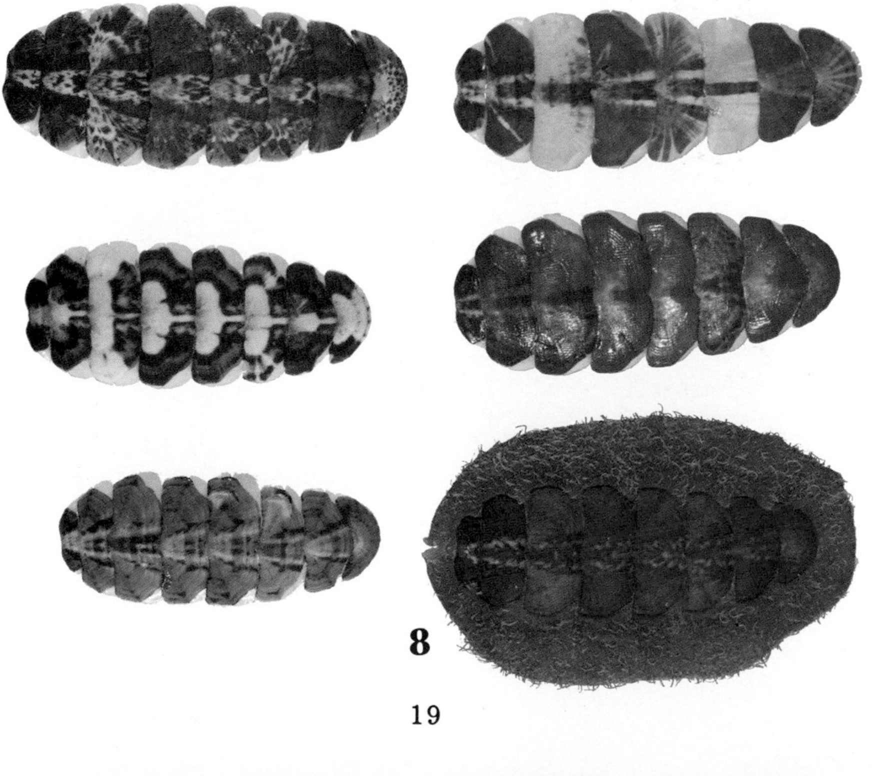

8

19

PLATE 3

7. *Mopalia swanii* Carpenter, 1864. Named in honor of the Reverend Swan, an early collector in the Neah Bay area of Washington. This chiton can be separated from the next by its velvety girdle, very sparcely strewn with small fine bristles. Uncommon from Alaska to northern California.

8. *Mopalia ciliata* Sowerby, 1840 can be distinguished from the above by its well-bristled girdle; the bristles resemble those of No. 6, but are much less course. Ranging from Alaska to northern Baja California it is not uncommon in the northern part of the range. Note the wide variations of color displayed in these two species.

PLATE 4

9. *Lepidozona mertensii* (Middendorff, 1846). Commonly red with whitish streaking, the girdle is covered with rounded scales usually arranged in patterns of reddish and white stripes. The sculpture features to note are rounded pustules on the head plate and lateral areas of the middle plates. Ranging uncommonly from Alaska to northern Baja California. Color variations go from solid maroon to a rare solid white.

10. *Lepidozona cooperi* Pilsbry, 1892 is usually solid gray in color and at first glance resembles No. 9 because of the same sculpturing; however, the girdle scales are noticeably coarse and heavily striated. Range is from Neah Bay to northern Baja California; uncommon.

11. *Mopalia species.* Reportedly under description at the present time, this can be distinguished from No. 7 and No. 8 by the complex girdle bristles and by the red flecks on the plates. Ranging from Alaska to central California; it is not common.

Plate 4

9

10

11

12

13

14

15

Plate 5

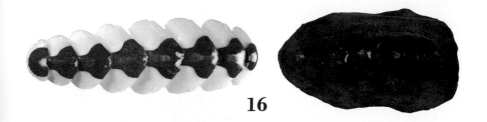

16

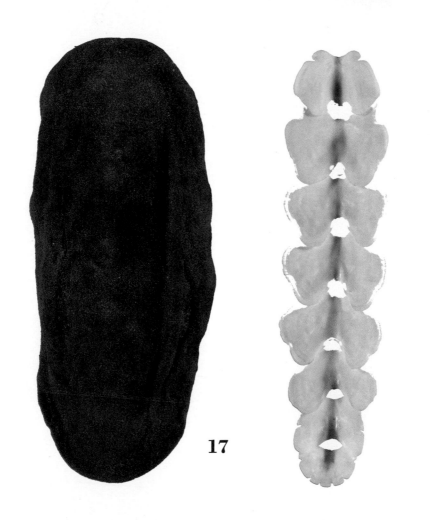

17

12. *Mopalia sinuata* Carpenter, 1864 can be separated from No. 13 by the girdle hairs which are shorter, heavier and with fairly heavy, curling spikes on each bristle. Alaska to Puget Sound, rare.

13. *Mopalia cirrata* Berry, 1919 in comparison with No. 12 the hairs of the girdle are longer and with finer branches. Alaska to northern California; rare.

14. *Placiphorella velata* Dall, 1879. **The Hooded Chiton** is easily identified by the fact that the girdle extends well forward of the nose plate. With its colorful "hood" it attracts tiny crustaceans which it smashes with the hood and eats! Range is from northern British Columbia to Baja California; rare.

15. *Cyanoplax dentiens* (Gould, 1846) is small, with finely punctate plate sculpture and a smooth-appearing girdle. Its position in the intertidal ranges from nearly the splash zone in exposed positions to bottoms of rocks at low tide. Fairly common from Alaska to central California.

PLATE 5 - Reduced to 1/2 Natural Size

16. *Katherina tunicata* (Wood, 1815). The well known **Black Katy** ranges from Alaska to central California. It is distinguished by the black, leathery girdle which covers all but a small portion of each plate. Common in the northern portion of its range.

17. *Cryptochiton stelleri* (Middendorff, 1846), the **Giant** or **Gumboot Chiton** is distinguished by its girdle completely covering all of the plates, as well as by its huge size—up to 14 inches! Not uncommon, usually in the subtidal, from Alaska to central California. Used by natives as food.

Gastropoda

Gastropoda are probably most diversified in their habitats of all shell life. There are several species of snails which inhabit the sand beaches, such as the moon snail and olives which can sometimes be collected on the surface, but which live burrowing along under the surface. The mud flats are the home of other species such as *Nassarius*, but for the most part, species of this Class prefer the rocky areas of the coastal and inland waters.

Habitats within this particular type of beach range from free-living forms under rocks, others crawling about in the open, some which live only near or on another animal (a shell-less local species lives in the intestines of the sea cucumber *Stichopus californicus*!) in a state of symbiosis or even as a parasite.

You might be somewhat surprised to learn that the size varies greatly also. Fully 90% of all species of Gastropods, in the adult size, never exceed a half inch! Our book has been limited to taking a look at those larger species one might encounter in the intertidal, with a few deeper water and small species included for reference.

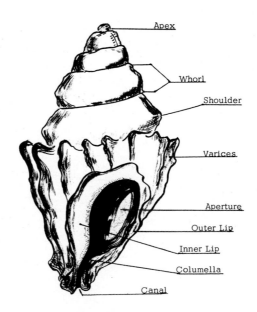

Plate 6

18

PLATE 6

18. *Haliotis kamtschatkana* Jonas, 1845. The **Pinto Abalone** ranges from the Siberian coast thru the northwest to central California. Living intertidally to 100 feet, it is found in rocky areas grazing on algae. Common in Alaska it becomes harder to find the further south you search.

PLATE 7

19. *Acmaea mitra* (Rathke, 1833). The **White-Cap Limpet** is found intertidally and to 75 feet on rocks from the Aleutians to Baja California. Common along most ocean beaches it is easily recognized by the conic shape and white color. The pinkish coloration is caused by a growth of coralline algae on the shell.

20. *Acmaea rosacea* Carpenter, 1864 is a tiny limpet which makes its home on growths of coralline algae in the intertidal zone and to depths of 20 feet. Not common from Ketchikan, Alaska to San Diego it can be distinguished by the small size, radiating color stripes and its habit of living on the coralline algae.

21. *Collisella digitalis* (Rathke, 1833). The **Finger Limpet** with a range from the Aleutians to Baja California is probably the most common of our limpets and most easily collected as it lives attached to rocks in the higher intertidal area. Note the ribs and the apex situated far forward.

22. *Collisella asmi* (Middendorff, 1847). The **Black Limpet** is most easily distinguished by its habit of living only on the shells of the Turban snails (see Plate 10). Occuring from British Columbia to southern Baja California it is no where common.

23. *Collisella strigatella* (Carpenter, 1864). (Synonym: *A. paradigitalis* Fritchman) This small limpet lives in the mid-intertidal area in or around tide pools from Vancouver Island to Guaymas, Mexico. Common in some areas.

Plate 7

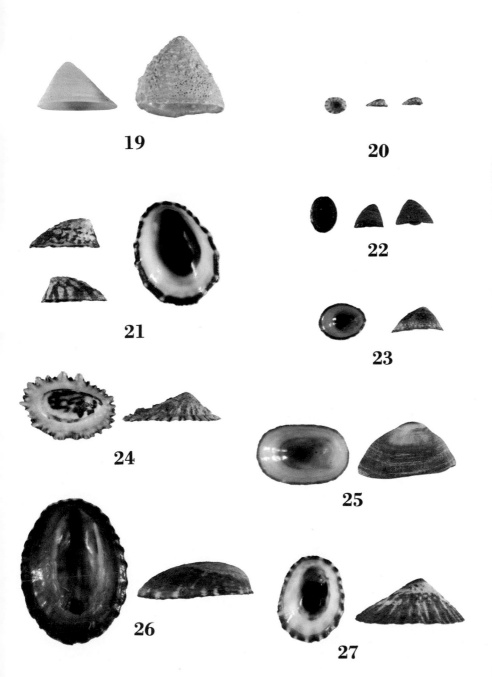

19

20

21

22

23

24

25

26

27

Plate 8

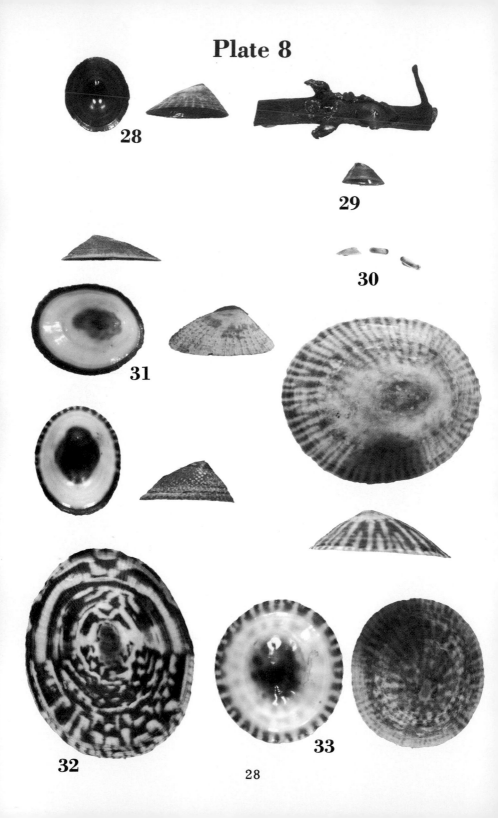

28

29

30

31

32

33

28

24. *Collisella scabra* (Gould, 1846). Vancouver Island to Mexico is the range of this uncommon species. Living in the intertidal zone it is distinguished by the many ribs which project past the edge of the shell.

25. *Collisella instabilis* (Gould, 1846). The **Kelp Limpet**. This interesting brown limpet lives attached to the stems of kelp from Kodiak Island to southern California. Though not uncommon it is usually collected from drift lines. Note the rectangular shape caused by its habitat on the kelp stem.

26. *Lottia gigantea* (Sowerby, 1834). The **Owl Limpet** has only recently been found in our area. Fairly large, living in the upper intertidal area attached to rocks, it is much more common in southern California and Baja. Note the odd-shaped internal brown spot and the low silhouette.

27. *Collisella pelta* (Rathke, 1833). Another common limpet found intertidally from the Aleutians to Baja California. Note its high conic shape and the numerous, though sometimes obsolete, ribs.

PLATE 8

28. *Notoacmaea fenestrata* (Reeve, 1855). **The Chocolate Limpet** ranges from Alaska to northern Baja California, making its home intertidally on rocks and boulders which are set in sand. This common species is distinguished easily by the chocolate color of the interior.

29. *Notoacmaea insessa* (Hinds, 1843). Intertidally from Wrangell, Alaska to central Baja California this limpet excavates a home on the kelp *Egregia* (Feather Boa). Not common, the color and habitat as well as size are features to note.

30. *Notoacmaea paleasea* (Gould, 1853). This tiny limpet lives on the blades of the open-coast eel grass

Phyllospadix from Vancouver Island to northern Baja though it is uncommon in our area. The tiny size and elongate-rectangular shape distinguish it.

31. *Collisella limatula* (Carpenter, 1864). The **File Limpet** is noted for the scales on its ribs. Living intertidally on rocks, possibly from Newport, Oregon to southern Baja California.

32. *Notoacmaea persona* (Rathke, 1833). This common intertidal species can be collected from Alaska to central California. The upper two figures are very typical, the lower represents an extremely large and colorful individual.

33. *Notoacmaea scutum* (Rathke, 1833). The **Plate Limpet** is another common form occuring in the intertidal on rocks from the Bering Sea to Baja California. Its flat, rounded shape and radiating color stripes are distinguishing features as well as its large size.

PLATE 9

34. *Diodora aspera* (Rathke, 1833). **Keyhole Limpets** are a common intertidal resident from Alaska to northern Baja, attached to rocks and on reef areas. The central hole in the apex and the brown stripes, though usually obscured somewhat by marine growths, are typical.

35. *Puncturella multistriata* Dall, 1914. An uncommon shell, this species is occasionally found intertidally and to 300 feet from Alaska to southern California. Attaches to rocks or dead shells.

36. *Puncturella galeata* (Gould, 1846). This uncommon shell lives in the subtidal to 300 foot depths from Alaska to Baja California. Its "hole" is located on the anterior slope of the shell and like No. 35 reminds one of the eye of a needle. Ribs are more numerous on this species than the previous one.

Plate 9

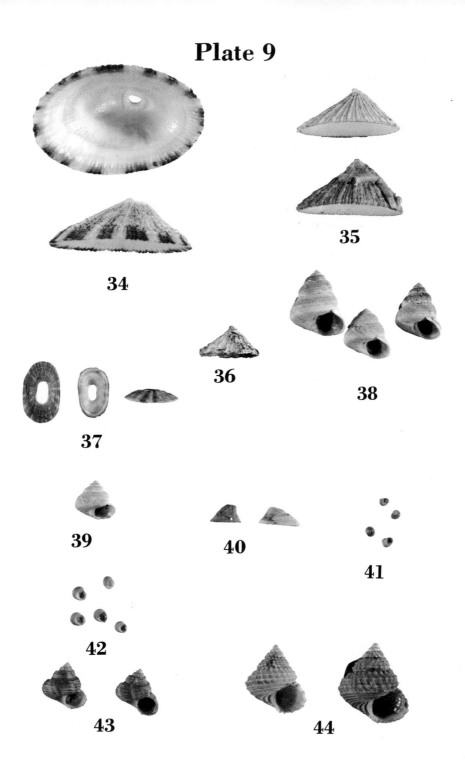

34

35

36

37

38

39

40

41

42

43

44

37. *Megatebennus bimaculatus* (Dall, 1871). Though not common this species occurs intertidally from southern Alaska to Baja California. Its large animal (nearly three times the size of the shell) lives under rocks and in crevices of the reef. Note the large central hole and the striped coloration.

38. *Margarites pupillus* (Gould, 1846). From Alaska to central California this common pinkish shell can be collected intertidally on reefs or under rocks. Size varies considerably between areas, but the shape and pinkish color are fairly constant.

39. *Margarites inflatulus* Dall, 1919. An uncommon species, occuring in depths of 100 to 750 feet. Vancouver Island and Puget Sound.

40. *Cryptobranchia concentrica* (Middendorff, 1847) is a limpet-shaped species which is uncommon from the Bering Sea to Puget Sound in subtidal to 200 foot depths where it attaches to stones or dead shells.

41. *Lirularia lirulata* (Carpenter, 1864) is a tiny species which seems more common just beyond the low tide area from Alaska to southern California; occasionally found intertidally. Coloration is of purplish-brown blotches on the silver shell.

42. *Lirularia succincta* (Carpenter, 1864). Common in both intertidal and subtidal zones of ocean beaches from the Gulf of Alaska to northern Baja California it lives under small rocks. The spiral sculpture and silver-gray color help separate this one.

43. *Solariella permabilis* Carpenter, 1864. Though this ranges from Alaska to southern California in 50 to 600 foot depths, it is not common.

44. *Cidarina cidaris* (A. Adams, 1864). From Alaska to southern California this species is found in depths of 150 to 1,000 feet. Not uncommon.

PLATE 10

45. *Calliostoma variegatum* Carpenter, 1864. Alaska to Baja California is the range of this uncommon species, from the intertidal to 600 foot depths.

46. *Calliostoma annulatum* (Lightfoot, 1786). This beautiful species, highly prized by collectors, is not common, though inhabiting the intertidal to 60 foot zone from Forrester Island, Alaska to northern Baja. The purplish tints on the yellowish shell and bright orange animal help separate this species.

47. *Calliostoma canaliculatum* (Lightfoot, 1786). Sitka, Alaska to Baja California in the intertidal to 600 foot depths, this uncommon species can be distinguished by its straight sides and even, revolving sculpture and by the yellowish color.

48. *Calliostoma ligatum* (Gould, 1846). **The Blue Top Shell** is the most common of this group and can be found amongst algae on and under rocks in the intertidal (to 750 foot) zone from Alaska to central California. The brick-red color, revolving sculpture and squat shape distinguish it from the others. The common name comes from specimens in which the outer layer of shell is worn away and the bluish pearl layer shows through.

49. *Calliostoma platinum* Dall, 1890. This rare species inhabits depths of 250 to 1,200 feet from the Queen Charlotte Islands to southern California. Note the lack of sculpture and waxy color. Much prized by collectors.

50. *Tegula brunnea* Philippi, 1848. The **Brown Turban** ranges intertidally from Oregon to southern California where it is not uncommon. The color and lack on an umbilicus are good features to look for.

51. *Tegula pulligo* (Gmelin, 1791). The **Northern Brown Turban** occurs from Alaska to Baja California, but is most common in the northern portion where it lives intertidally amongst the rocks and tide pools. Note the light base and the umbilicus.

52. *Tegula funebralis* (A. Adams, 1855). The very common **Black Turban** lives intertidally from the Queen Charlotte Islands to central Baja California where it feeds on decaying algae amongst the rocks and in tide pools. Blackish-purple color and light tip separate this species from others in the group.

PLATE 11

53. *Littorina scutulata* Gould, 1849. The **Checkered Periwinkle** is not always as colorful as these, but the checkered appearance is visible. Very common from Alaska to Baja California this species lives high in the intertidal on rocks amongst barnacles.

54. *Littorina planaxis* Philippi, 1847. Ranging from Oregon to southern Baja California this dull-colored species is distinguished by its flattened columellar area.

55. *Littorina sitkana* Philippi, 1845. **Sitka Periwinkles** range from the Bering Sea to Puget Sound and are very common in the high and mid intertidal areas. More colorful than the last species this is usually more highly sculptured as well.

56. *Lacuna marmorata* Dall, 1919. Common from Alaska to San Diego this species is found on kelp and other algae in the intertidal zone.

57. *Lacuna porrecta* Carpenter, 1864 is found more often in the coastal bays and open coast areas from Alaska to Baja California. It too lives on various algaes in the intertidal zone.

Plate 10

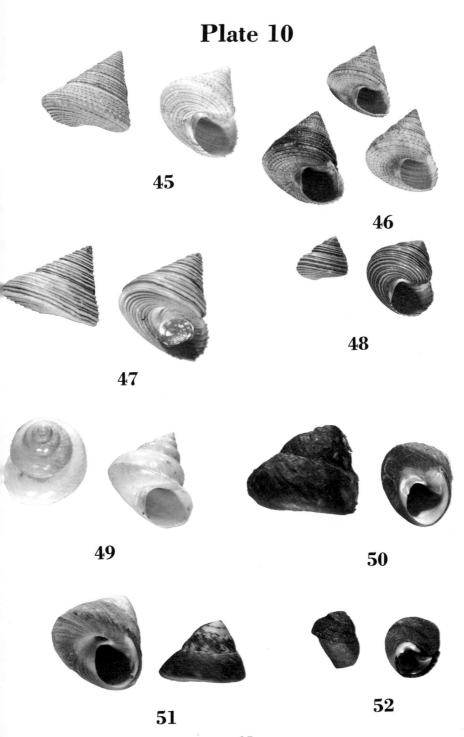

45

46

47

48

49

50

51

52

58. *Lacuna carinata* Gould, 1848. Common from Alaska to southern California on various species of intertidal algaes.

59. *Tricolia pulloides* Carpenter, 1864. Because of its small size this is easily overlooked in the intertidal zone from Puget Sound to Baja California where it lives on the undersides of rocks and amongst pinkish coralline algae. Not common this can be distinguished by the stony, pearl-green operculum.

60. *Homalopoma luridum* (Dall, 1885). (Synonym: *H. carpenteri*). Ranging from northern British Columbia to Baja California this reddish, purplish or grayish shell has a stony white operculum and inhabits the intertidal zone under rocks. Common.

61. *Astraea gibberosa* (Dillwyn, 1817). From the Queen Charlotte Islands to San Diego this uncommon shell can be found from the intertidal zone to depths of 100 feet, amongst rocks and algae. Note the brick-red color, the sculptured base and especially the large stony operculum. Large adults usually have broken tips and are overgrown with various marine animals and plants.

PLATE 12

62. *Batillaria zonalis* (Bruguière, 1792). An introduced species from Japan this has become established in various muddy bays in our area. Very common where found and unlikely to be mistaken for anything else. It seems to prefer mud flats.

63. *Cerithiopsis species*. Presented as a representative of a number of small gastropods belonging to this group. Intertidal on undersides of rocks which are bedded in mud or gravel. See No. 157 also.

Plate 11

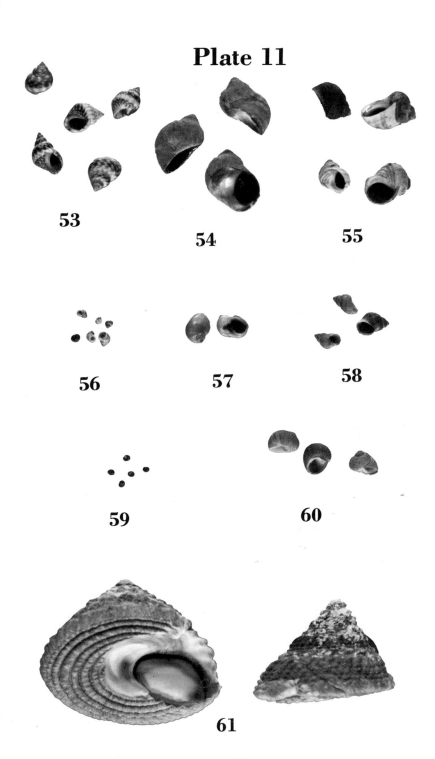

53

54

55

56

57

58

59

60

61

64. *Bittium subplanatum* (Carpenter, 1864). Found in the subtidal to 300 foot depths from Puget Sound to San Diego this not uncommon snail can be distinguished by the chalky color and texture of the shell.

65. *Bittium eschrichtii* (Middendorff, 1849). Very common from Alaska to the Washington coast this small snail lives intertidally amongst rocks in gravel.

66. *Bittium eschrichtii ?icelum* Bartsch, 1907. A possible subspecies of the above, this occurs from Puget Sound to central California and is noted for the deeply incised sculpture.

67. *Tachyrynchus lacteolus* (Carpenter, 1864). An uncommon species occuring from the intertidal to 300 foot depths and ranging from Alaska to Baja California, the vertical sculpturing is its most identifying feature.

68. *Hipponix cranoides* Carpenter, 1864. **The Horse's Hoof** lives on the undersides of rocks and in crevices and empty burrows in soft stone, intertidally and to 15 feet. Range is from British Columbia to Oregon. Note the limpet-like shape and the odd muscle scar in the interior.

69. *Calyptraea fastigiata* Gould, 1846. The **Chinese Hat** is not uncommon from Alaska to Puget Sound where it lives attached to stones or dead shells from the intertidal to 300 foot depths. Note the limpet-like shape, but with a shelf on the inside.

70. *Crepidula perforans* Valenciennes, 1846. This **Slipper Shell** is common from northern British Columbia to Baja California where it lives intertidally (and to 15 feet) attached to rocks (the lower pair) or in the apertures of dead snail shells (the upper pair). Sometimes mislabelled *C. nummaria* Gould.

Plate 12

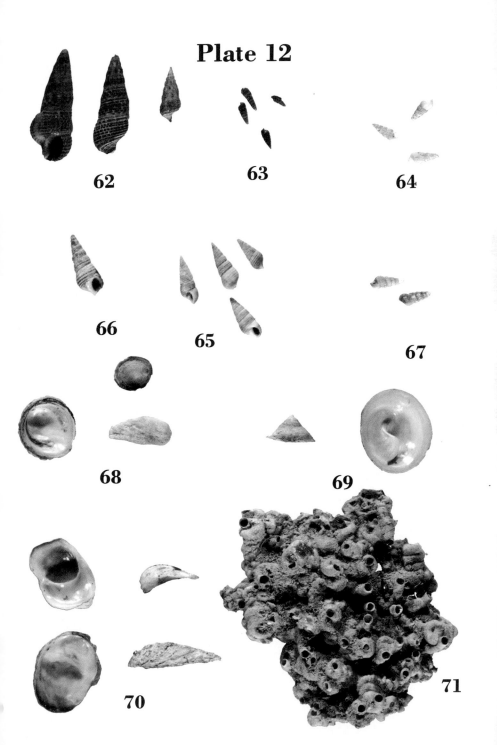

62

63

64

66

65

67

68

69

70

71

71. *Vermetus compactus* Carpenter, 1864. This rare species occasionally is found on the underside of ledges in the intertidal zone from Vancouver Island to southern California. Always occurs in worm-like clusters.

PLATE 13

72. *Crepidula fornicata* (Linné, 1758). The **Atlantic Slipper** is another of our accidentally introduced species found in certain areas of this coast. Note the speckled coloring and the habit of piling up in stacks. Common in or near commercial oyster beds.

73. *Crepipatella lingulata* (Gould, 1846). The **Half-Slipper Shell** occurs from Alaska to central Mexico in the intertidal zone and to depths of 120 feet where it attaches to rocks or dead shells. The common name refers to the internal shelf which does not completely cross the width of the shell.

74. *Crepidula adunca* Sowerby, 1825 is called the **Hooked Slipper** and is found attached to other gastropod shells hitching a free ride in the intertidal area (and to 60 feet deep). Common from the Queen Charlotte Islands to northern Baja California. Note the chocolate color and the little hooked apex.

75. *Trichotropis cancellata* Hinds, 1843. This odd little shell can sometimes be found in the very low intertidal and to 150 foot depths from Alaska to Oregon. Living among sea squirts or tube worms it can be distinguished by the hairy periostracum and cancellate sculpture.

Plate 13

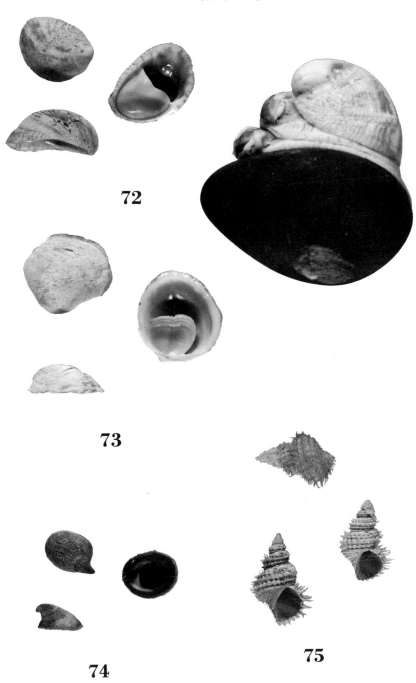

72

73

74

75

41

Plate 14

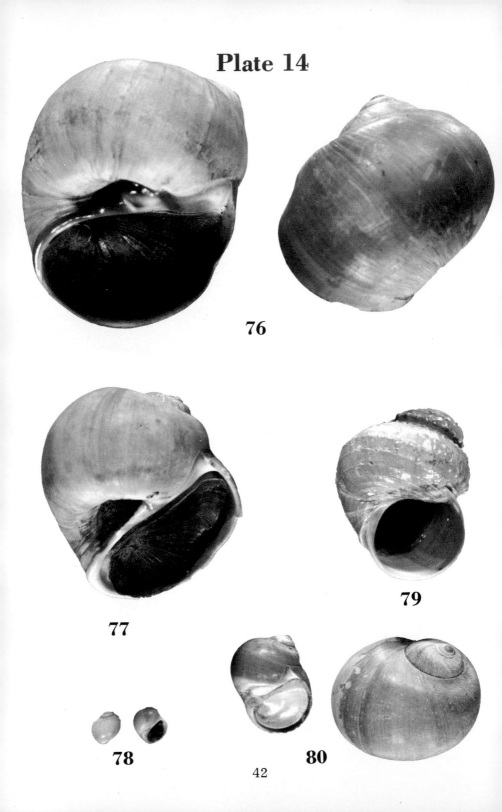

76

77

79

78

80

PLATE 14

76. *Polinices lewisii* (Gould, 1847). The **Northern** or **Lewis's Moon Snail** is the largest species of this group found anywhere, reaching a length of nearly six inches! Common on sand flats from the Queen Charlottes to northern Baja California (rare in the south) in the intertidal to 150 feet deep this gastropod burrows along under the sand searching out bivalves to eat.

77. *Polinices draconis* (Dall, 1903). This rare deepwater species (300 to 1,000 feet) is distinguished from the above by the wide-open, deep umbilicus. The range is from Alaska to Baja California.

78. *Polinices pallida* Broderip & Sowerby, 1829. This small moon snail is found from 60 to 600 feet deep from Alaska to central California and is not common anywhere. The lack of an umbilicus, the yellowish periostracum and horny operculum help distinguish this form from small specimens of the other moon snails.

79. *Bathybembix bairdii* (Dall, 1889). A rare deepwater shell (600 to 4,000 feet deep), this is most closely related to species No. 44. Ranging from Alaska to Baja California it is a prized collector's species.

80. *Natica clausa* Broderip & Sowerby, 1829. Though not common this snail can be found from the intertidal to depths of 600 feet from the Bering Sea to Baja California. Living in the sand it's distinguishing features include the lack of an umbilicus, a large callus pad, and the hard, stony operculum.

PLATE 15

81. *Opalia chacei* Strong, 1937. Not uncommon, this shell ranges from British Columbia possibly to Guaymas, Mexico, intertidally and to depths of 50 feet. It lives near small anemones (in gravel) from

which it sucks it food. All wentletraps (this includes this species and Nos. 82, 84-88) can extrude a purplish dye when disturbed.

82. *Epitonium grönlandicum* (Perry, 1811). This rare deepwater shell (300 to 1,000 feet) ranges, in the Pacific, from the Bering Sea to British Columbia; it also occurs in the Atlantic. Note the sculpturing between the varices.

83. *Balcis micans* (Carpenter, 1864). This sharp-spired, shiny shell occurs intertidally and to a depth of 60 feet from British Columbia to Baja California but is not common.

84. *Epitonium indianorum* (Carpenter, 1864). Not common, and a collector's prize, this beautiful wentletrap can be found from the intertidal to 600 foot depths from Alaska to Baja California. No. 88 is the same species.

85. *Epitonium ?sawinae* Dall, 1903 is a rare species occasionally found in the intertidal zone, it ranges from Vancouver Island to Catalina Island, Calif.

86. *Epitonium tinctum* (Carpenter, 1864). Another rare species, this occurs from the intertidal to depths of 1,300 feet from Vancouver Island to the Gulf of California.

87. *Epitonium montereyensis* Dall, 1907. Yet another rare species of this group, ranging from Vancouver Island to southern California.

88. Same as No. 84.

89. *Lamellaria stearnsii* Dall, 1871. From Alaska to Baja California this shell lives from the intertidal zone to depths of 60 feet on a black-speckled white compound, ascidian, usually on the underside of ledges. The animal is larger than the shell and is the color of the ascidian.

Plate 15

81

82

83

84

85

86

87

88

89

90

91

45

Plate 16

92

93

90. *Velutina prolongata* Carpenter, 1864. The rarer of the two species of this genus one finds in this area, this species in shiny appearing and lacks sculpturing. Ranging from Alaska to central California this occurs from the intertidal to 150 feet deep.

91. *Velutina laevigata* (Linné, 1767). Though not common, this does occur in the intertidal zone and to depths of 60 feet on the undersides of ledges and among ascidians. Alaska to central California is the range of this sculptured species.

PLATE 16

92. *Fusitriton oregonensis* (Redfield, 1848) is the **Oregon Triton** and is an impressive shell with a long range from Japan and Alaska to Baja California. Found intertidally, and to 300 feet deep amongst rocks, the hairy periostracum and cancellate sculpture as well as its size are good features to note.

93. *Ceratostoma foliata* (Gmelin, 1792). The **Leafy Hornmouth** is another of the more spectacular shells of our region, ranging from Alaska to San Diego in the intertidal and to depths of 150 feet. It is distinguished by the wing-like varices (sometimes not too well developed) and a tooth on the outer lip of the aperture. The two small specimens here show the normal coloration of the species.

PLATE 17

94. *Ocenebra sclera* (Dall, 1919). This pretty shell ranges from British Columbia to Washington and lives intertidally on the sides and bottoms of rocks. Not common; note the large size compared to others of this group and the dark markings between the varices.

95. *Ocenebra interfossa* (Carpenter, 1864). Intertidal on rocks and in crevices amongst gravel from Alaska to Baja California. This sharp-shouldered shell with cancellate sculpture is not common.

96. *Ocenebra atropurpurea* (Carpenter, 1865) ranges from the Queen Charlotte Islands to northern Baja California from the intertidal to 100 feet on rocks and in crevices amongst barnacles. Not common.

97. *Ocenebra lurida* (Middendorff, 1849). Very common, this variable little shell lives in the intertidal zone from Sitka, Alaska to Baja California. The color varies from yellow to orange, to brown and to purplish-brown with occasional specimens displaying stripes. The sculpture of incised lines is a good feature for identification.

98. Same species as No. 95.

99. *Ocenebra japonica* (Dunker, 1860). The **Japanese Oyster Drill**, since its accidental introduction to Puget Sound and British Columbia, has become a real pest to the commercial oyster grower, as it likes nothing better than to eat small oysters. The wing-like varices are not always so well-developed as in these specimens; also note the different appearance of the juvenile specimen in the center with the numbers written on the columella.

PLATE 18

100. *Trophonopsis lasius* (Dall, 1919). This shell is not common, but ranges in the intertidal to 500 foot depths from Alaska to central California and is sought after by the collector. The long straight canal and cancellate sculpture with the white color are distinguishing features.

101. *Urosalpinx cinereus* Say, 1822. The **Eastern Oyster Drill** is rather hard to find in our area as it only occurs where attempts have been made to establish the eastern oyster *(Ostrea virginia)*. Its orange colored aperture and nearly obsolete sculpture helps identify it.

Plate 17

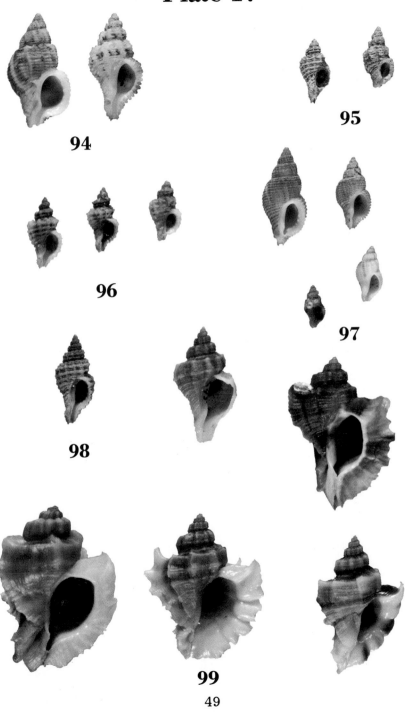

94

95

96

97

98

99

102. *Trophon pacificus* Dall, 1902. This beautiful little shell is uncommon in depths of 50 to 400 feet from Alaska to Mexico and can be identified by the continuous varices and its narrow, elongate form.

103. *Trophon multicostatus* Eschscholtz, 1829. One of the sought-after *Trophon* group, this beauty ranges from Alaska to southern California from the intertidal zone to depths of 150 feet and is recognized by its sharp shoulders with the varices nearly producing spines where they intersect.

104. *Thais canaliculata* (Duclos, 1832) has deeply channeled sculpturing to distinguish it from others of this group. This intertidal snail, which lives on rocks amongst the barnacles from Alaska to central California, is extremely variable as to color.

105. *Thais emarginata* (Deshayes, 1839), the **Dogwinkle**, is very common on rocky shores from the Bering Sea to Baja California. Note the short canal and almost lack of sculpture as well as the wide range of color.

106. *Thais lima* (Gmelin, 1791) is common in the intertidal zone amongst the barnacles from Alaska to at least Puget Sound. This should be compared with No. 104 from which it differs in being slightly more squat and its sculpture more numerous and not so deeply incised.

107. *Acanthina spirata* (Blainville, 1832), though rare in our area, is fairly common in southern California. It lives in the intertidal and to depths of 75 feet on rocks and can be distinguished by its coloration and a sharp tooth on its outer lip.

Plate 18

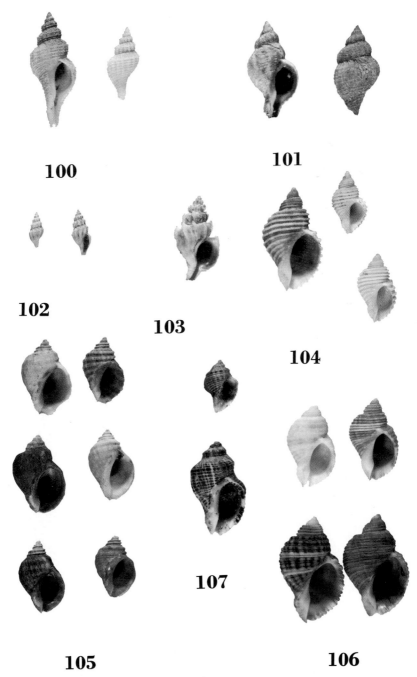

100

101

102

103

104

105

107

106

51

Plate 19

108

52

PLATE 19

108. *Thais lamellosa* (Gmelin, 1791). Probably the most variable shell on our coast, this species is common on nearly every beach where there are at least a few rocks. The sculpture ranges from smooth to numerous wrinkled varices and the color from white to orange and brown and all shades and striping combinations. It ranges from Alaska to central California in the intertidal and to depths of nearly 400 feet. Featured on our cover.

PLATE 20 - Specimens shown at 1/2 Natural Size.

109. *Beringius eyerdami* A. G. Smith, 1959. This uncommon, deepwater shell (60 to 600 foot depths) ranges from the Queen Charlotte Islands to Puget Sound. The large size, tabled shoulders and incised sculpture are constants. Named for Walter J. Eyerdam, noted Seattle naturalist.

110. *Boreomelon stearnsii* (Dall, 1872). The **Alaska Volute** is probably the most valuable species shown in this book. It ranges from Alaska to the Queen Charlotte Islands in depths of 200 to 1,000 and more feet. Note the smoothly flowing shape and the folds on the columella.

111. *Neptunea cf. pribiloffensis* (Dall, 1919). Another of of the uncommon shells brought up from deepwater (500 to 4,000 feet) from the Pribiloff Islands to the Washington coast.

112. *Neptunea smirnia* (Dall, 1919) is an uncommon shell ranging from Alaska to the Washington coast in depths of 200 to 4,000 feet.

113. *Neptunea ithia* (Dall, 1891). From deep water (500 to 4,000 feet) off Oregon and northern California. Rare.

114. *Neptunea phoeniceus* (Dall, 1891). Uncommon, from Alaska to the Oregon coast in depths of 400 to 4,000 feet.

115. *Neptunea tabulata* (Baird, 1863). This pagoda-shaped species lives in depths of 60 to 1,000 feet from the Queen Charlotte Islands to San Diego and is probably most common of all the *Neptunea* of our coast.

116. *Neptunea lirata* (Gmelin, 1791). Found in 150 to 1,000 foot depths from the Bering Sea to Baja California this species has also been brought into the intertidal zone by hermit crabs on occasion.

117. *Neptunea stilesi* A. G. Smith, 1968. Named in honor of the late Everett Stiles of Bellingham, Washington, this species occurs in 60 to 600 feet from northern British Columbia to the Washington coast.

PLATE 21

118. *Exilioidea rectirostris* (Carpenter, 1864). Rare. From Alaska to Oregon, this has been taken in depths of 250 to 1,500 feet.

119. *Searlesia dira* (Reeve, 1846) is the **Dire Whelk** and a common intertidal dweller amongst the rocks and gravel or near sea urchins. It ranges from southern Alaska to southern California.

120. *Buccinum plectrum* Stimpson, 1855, ranges from Point Barrow, Alaska to the Washington coast in depths of 100 to 2,000 feet. Uncommon.

121. Same as No. 120.

122. *Buccinum strigillatum* Dall, 1891 is a fairly common deepwater species ranging from the Queen Charlotte Islands to Baja California in depths of 250 to 4,500 feet.

Plate 20

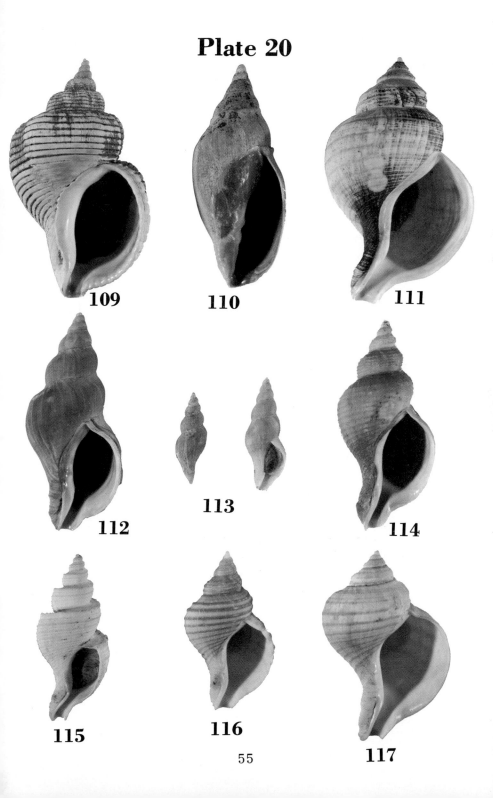

109

110

111

112

113

114

115

116

55

117

123. *Colus jordani* Dall, 1913 is not common, but occasionally collected in depths of 150 to 6,000 feet from the Bering Sea to central California.

124. *Colus errones* Dall, 1919. Uncommon in depths of 600 to 6,000 feet from the Pribiloff Islands to the coast of Washington.

125. *Colus morditus* Dall, 1919 ranges only along the coasts of British Columbia and Washington in depths of 360 to 6,000 feet; uncommon.

126. *Colus halli* (Dall, 1873) is not common in depths of 600 to 6,000 feet from the Bering Sea to southern California.

PLATE 22

127. *Ilyanassa obsoleta* (Say, 1822). Introduced into various areas from British Columbia to San Francisco where eastern oysters have been planted. Living intertidally on mud flats, the chocolate color and pitted appearance distinguish the species.

128. *Nassarius perpingius* (Hinds, 1844) is found from the intertidal area to depths of 60 feet from the Queen Charlotte Islands to Baja California. This uncommon species is distinguished by its fine cancellate sculpture and yellowish color.

129. *Nassarius fossatus* (Gould, 1849). The orange-colored aperture and large size separate this intertidal mud flat resident. Ranging from the Queen Charlotte Islands to Baja California it is not common in our area though dead specimens can be found in many areas.

130. *Nassarius cooperi* (Forbes, 1850) ranges in the subtidal (and to depths of 100 feet) from Puget Sound to San Diego. Not uncommon it can be distinguished by the sharp ribs.

Plate 21

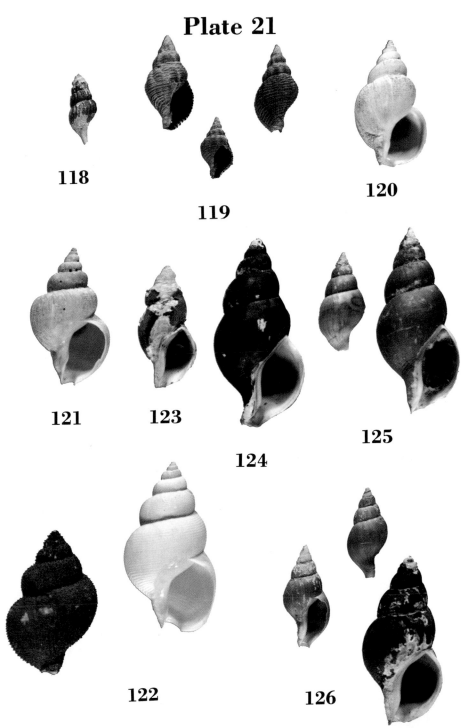

118

119

120

121

123

124

125

122

126

131. *Nassarius mendicus* (Gould, 1849), the **Lean Basket Snail**, ranges from Kodiak Island, Alaska to central Baja California on the mud and sand flats from the intertidal zone to depths of 30 feet. It can be separated from the above form by its tall, slender shape and lower, less-defined ribbing. Very common.

132. *Mitrella gouldii* (Carpenter, 1856). This white-dotted little shell can be collected in the subtidal, to 600 feet, from northern British Columbia to Baja California. Common on sand or mud bottoms.

133. *Mitrella carinata* (Hinds, 1844), the common **Dove Shell**, is a part of the population under rocks and on sand/mud bottoms in the intertidal and to depths of 50 feet. The range is Alaska to Mexico.

134. *Amphissa columbiana* Dall, 1916. Ranging from Alaska to southern California this common species is found on rocks from the intertidal zone to depths of 150 feet.

135. *Oenopota species.* Taken off Vancouver Island in 200 feet.

136. *Nassarius fraticularis* (Bruguière, 1789) is another of the accidentally introduced species from Japan which has become established in some muddy bays of our area. The bright coloration and sharp shoulders distinguish it from the natives.

PLATE 23

137. *Fusinus harfordii* (Stearns, 1871). Our only representative of this more tropical group of spindle shells, this ranges from the northern tip of Vancouver Island to central California. Uncommon everywhere, it lives from the intertidal to depths of 50 feet on rocks and is usually somewhat encrusted with lime growths.

Plate 22

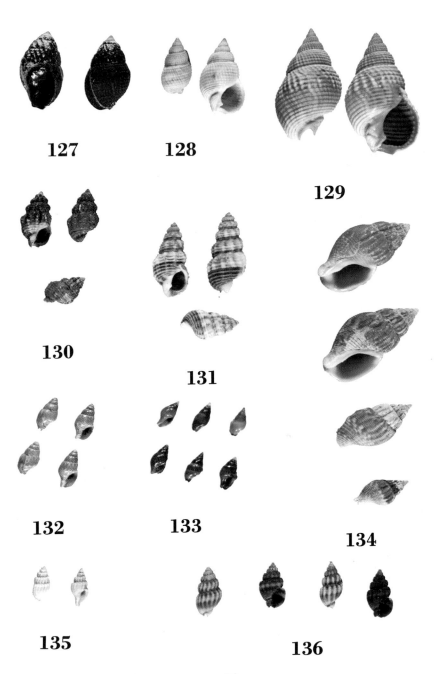

127

128

129

130

131

132

133

134

135

136

138. *Antiplanes perversa* (Gabb, 1865) shouldn't be mistaken for anything else as this is our only large gastropod twisted in the opposite direction from normal. This left-handed species occurs in depths of 150 to 1,500 feet from northern British Columbia to Mexico.

139. *Olivella biplicata* (Sowerby, 1825), the **Purple Olive**, lives on sand flats where it moves along just beneath the surface. Ranging from Sitka, Alaska to Baja California this common snail is usually bluish-purple or gray; the uncommon color forms of brown, pink and white illustrate the great color variation.

140. *Olivella baetica* Carpenter, 1864, the **Brown Olive**, ranges from Kodiak Island, Alaska to Baja California and is not uncommon from the intertidal to depths of 100 feet on sand bottoms. The smaller size, brownish color with white maculations distinguish this from the above.

141. *Oenopota fidicula* (Gould, 1849) ranges from Alaska to Puget Sound in depths of 50 to 600 feet.

PLATE 24

142. *Granulina margaritula* (Carpenter, 1857). Ranging from Alaska to Panama, this common (if you know where to look) little snail lives from the intertidal zone to depths of 150 feet on rocks amongst tube worms as well as coralline algae. The small, shiny, egg-shape mark the species. The animal completely covers the shell when living and is yellowish or pinkish in color.

143. *Oenopota species*. Though subtidal this unidentified species can occasionally be collected from drift lines along the open coast.

Plate 23

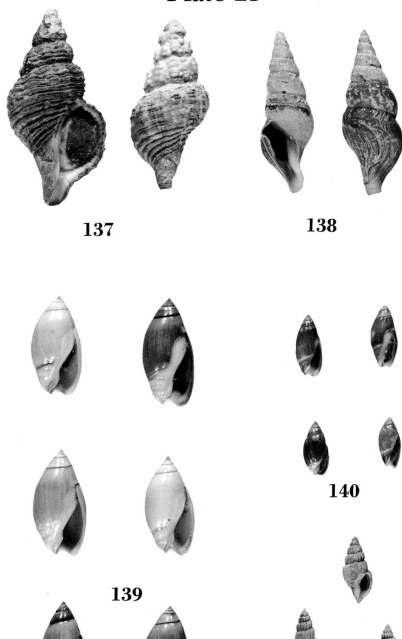

137

138

139

140

141

144. *Oenopota tabulata* (Carpenter, 1864) ranges from Alaska to central California in depths of 50 to 250 feet. Uncommon.

145. *Mangelia angulata* Carpenter, 1864. Another subtidal (to 300 feet) shell, this one is uncommonly collected from Alaska to Baja California. Included to illustrate the genus which is well represented in our area. See No. 149 also.

146. *Oenopota species*. Another of this group of small gastropods.

147. *Fartulum occidentale* Bartsch, 1920 is a tube-shaped snail, not uncommon from the subtidal to 150 foot depths from Alaska to central Baja California.

148. *Acteocina eximia* (Baird, 1863). This bubble shell or barrel shell is found from the intertidal to depths of 150 feet in sand and its range is from southern Alaska to Puget Sound; not common.

149. *Mangelia species*. See discussion under No. 145.

150. *Caecum crebricinctum* (Carpenter, 1864). Not uncommon in gravel from the intertidal to 300 feet with a range of Alaska to Baja California. Another of the odd little tube-shaped gastropods like No. 147.

151. *Acteon punctocaelata* Carpenter, 1864. This purplish-brown striped little bubble shell occurs on sand or mud bottoms from Ketchikan, Alaska to Baja California. Uncommon in the intertidal and to depths of 150 feet.

152. *Turbonilla species*. Included here to illustrate another of the groups of small gastropods. These are separated by the sculpturing, which is vertical.

153. *Iselica fenestrata* (Carpenter, 1864) is not common, though found from the Queen Charlotte Islands to

Plate 24

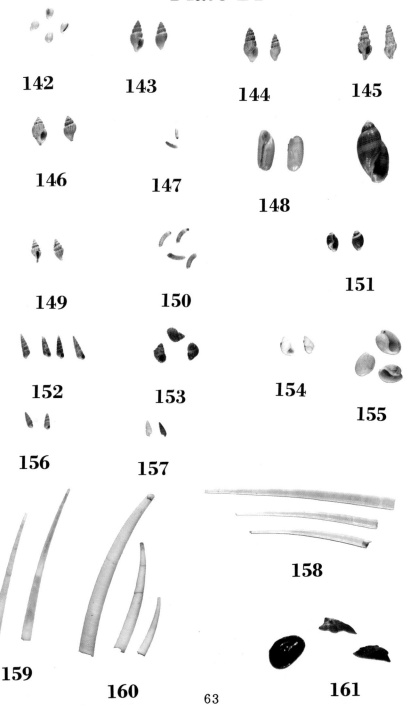

142

143

144

145

146

147

148

149

150

151

152

153

154

155

156

157

158

159

160

161

Baja California where it lives intertidally amongst the byssus threads of mussels.

154. *Odostomia angularis* Dall and Bartsch, 1907. Though found in the drift this species lives in depths of 50 to 150 feet from Vancouver Island to central California. Used here to illustrate this genus which is represented in our area by a dozen or more species.

155. *Haminoea vesicula* Gould, 1853, a **Bubble Shell**, found commonly in the intertidal area amongst eel grass on sand or mud flats from Ketchikan, Alaska to central Baja California.

156. *Turbonilla species*, see No. 152.

157. *Cerithiopsis species*, see No. 63.

158. *Dentalium dalli* Pilsbry and Sharp, 1897. One of the deepwater tusk shells, this species ranges from the Bering Sea to Mexico in depths of 300 to 3,000 feet. Rare.

159. *Dentalium rectius* Carpenter, 1864 is a transparent, extremely fragile and rare species which occurs in depths of 60 to 600 feet from Alaska to Panama.

160. *Dentalium pretiosum* Sowerby, 1860. The **Money Tusk** (or **Wampum**), was used as currency by the Indians of our area and has been collected in depths of 30 to 250 feet from northern British Columbia to San Diego, though it is uncommon throughout the range.

161. *Siphonaria thersites* Carpenter, 1864 is actually an air-breathing limpet-like gastropod which lives from mid to high intertidal amongst the bladderwrack seaweed from Alaska to Oregon. Uncommon.

Pelecypoda

I think everyone knows that clams or bivalves (the Pelecypoda) live, in most cases, buried in sand or mud bottoms. These can be collected by using a simple shovel, but here again remember to put back any sand or mud you remove in your search. There are species of bivalves which attach themselves to rocks, pilings, other shells and still others which can be collected from their burrows in limestone, clay, other shells or wood. One small local species even attaches itself to the belly of the worm known as the "sea mouse". The group known as scallops lives a free-swimming existence. Various habitats are noted under the various species in the text.

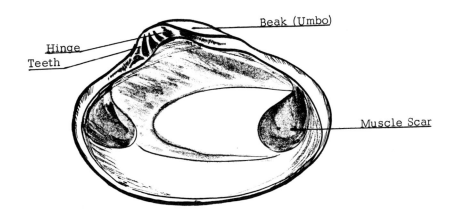

65

Plate 25

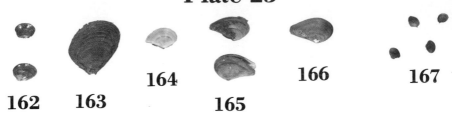

162   163   164   165   166   167

168   169   170

171   172

173   174   175

PLATE 25

162. *Nucula tenuis* (Montagu, 1808). Not common in depths of 30 to 600 feet from the Bering Sea to San Diego.

163. *Acila castrensis* (Hinds, 1845). The **Tent Nut Clam** lives on mud or sand bottoms in depths of 50 to 750 feet from Alaska to Baja California. Note the chevron or tent-shaped markings; not uncommon.

164. *Nuculana hamata* (Carpenter, 1864) is uncommonly found in depths of 300 to 600 feet from northern British Columbia to Panama.

165. *Nuculana minuta* (Fabricius, 1776). Not uncommon in depths of 50 to 300 feet from the Arctic Ocean to San Diego.

166. *Nuculana acuta* (Conrad, 1832) is a species occuring from Alaska to Baja California in depths of 600 to 6,000 feet; rare.

167. *Crenella decussata* (Montagu, 1808). Common on sandy or mud bottoms in depths of 30 to 300 feet from Alaska to San Diego.

168. *Yoldia beringiana* Dall, 1916 is collected from the Pribiloff Islands to British Columbia in depths of 300 to 6,000 feet; rare.

169. *Yoldia scissurata* Dall, 1897, is an uncommon species living in depths of 100 to 1,200 feet from Alaska to southern California.

170. *Glycymeris subobsoleta* (Carpenter, 1864) is another uncommon inhabitant of the subtidal zone and depths to 250 feet. Range is from northern British Columbia to San Diego; note the numerous teeth on the hinge.

Plate 26

176   **177**

181   **180**

178

182

179

68

171. *Mytilus californianus* Conrad, 1837. The common **Sea Mussel** lives attached to rocks along the ocean beaches in the intertidal zone from the Aleutian Islands to southern Baja. The ribbing and large size, up to ten inches, are notable.

172. *Mytilus edulis* Linné, 1758. The **Edible** or **Blue Mussel** occurs in waters around the world, from the intertidal to depths of 120 feet where it attaches to pilings, rocks, etc., usually in quieter waters than the last species. It lacks the sculpture of the previous mussel; also note the two color forms.

173. *Modiolus modiolus* (Linné, 1757), is not uncommon, attached to rocks and pilings in the intertidal zone from Alaska to Baja California. The numerous hairs on the periostracum and color separate this from allied species.

174. *Musculus substriatus* (Gray, 1824) is found in the subtidal to depths of 600 feet from Alaska to Puget Sound. On sand bottoms in self-made "nest" of agglutinated sand or attached to sea squirts.

175. *Musculus senhousi* (Reeve, 1847) is another accidental introduction to Puget Sound with Japanese oyster spat. Attached to rocks and shells in the intertidal zone in or near commercial oyster beds.

PLATE 26

176. *Adula falcata* (Gould, 1851). This little mussel lives in holes bored in soft limstone from Coos Bay, Oregon to Baja California and is separable from the next species by its netted sculpture. Not uncommon.

177. *Adula californiensis* (Philippi, 1847), is called the **Date Mussel,** and also lives in bores in limestone but ranges from Vancouver Island to San Diego. Not uncommon this lacks the sculpture of No. 176. Both species are found in the intertidal zone.

178. *Pododesmus macroschisma* (Deshayes, 1839). The **Jingle** shell lives attached to the undersides, sides and tops of rocks, on pilings, inside dead bivalves, from northern British Columbia to southern California. Common from the intertidal to depths of 60 feet. Note the hole in the lower valve through which the animal thrusts a muscle to attach itself to its home.

179. *Bankia setacea* Tryon, 1863 is known also as the **Teredo** or **Ship Worm** and is infamous for its destruction of many wooden structures which come in contact with the sea. Common from the intertidal to depths of 100 feet the bivalve shells at the left do the burrowing and at the other end of its limy tubes are the palletes (right) which help circulate water through the tube.

180. *Delectopecten vancouverensis* (Whiteaves, 1893) is found uncommonly from northern British Columbia to San Diego in depths of 30 to 1,200 feet on sand or mud bottoms sometimes attached to objects. Under magnification small scales or spines are visible.

181. *Delectopecten tillamookensis* (Arnold, 1906) is a deepwater (1,000 to 3,000 feet) resident from Vancouver Island to Baja California. Note the net-like sculpturing on this rare species.

182. *Hinnites giganteus* (Gray, 1825) see discussion for next plate.

PLATE 27 - Lower figure 1/2 Natural Size.

182. *Hinnites giganteus* (Gray, 1825) is commonly called the **Rock Scallop** because as an adult it attaches itself to rocks in the intertidal to 100 foot zone from Alaska to Baja California. Before permanently settling down the shells can swim from place to place. The figures on Plate 26 and the upper left figure on this plate are juvenile, free-swimming stages. You can see the imprint of the juvenile

Plate 27

182

183

Plate 28

184

185

186

stage near the hinge of the large adult on this plate. Most adults are very worm-eaten and heavily encrusted, they sometimes reach a diameter of 10 inches. The muscle is delicious !

183. *Pecten caurinus* Gould, 1850, the **Weathervane Scallop**, is the largest species of scallop in the world reaching 12 inches in diameter! It occurs in depths of 15 to 450 feet from southern Alaska to Oregon and is locally common. Juvenile on the upper left.

PLATE 28

184. *Chlamys hericia* (Gould, 1850), also called the **Pacific Pink Scallop**,, is not uncommon from northern British Columbia to Oregon in the intertidal to 600 foot zone. Adults are free-swimming while juveniles occasionally attach themselves to rocks or algae. Sculpture less regular than No. 185 and this has fewer ribs than does No. 186. The ribs are covered with tiny spines.

185. *Chlamys hastata* (Sowerby, 1842) has a habitat identical with the last species, but ranges from northern British Columbia to Baja California. The brightly flushed interior seems to be an identifying feature.

186. *Chlamys rubidus* (Hinds, 1845) (Synonym: *C. hindsii* Carpenter). Living in depths of 30 to 300 feet from Alaska to central California, this colorful species can be separated by the lack of spines on the ribs. Not common.

PLATE 29

187. *Meretrix meretrix* Röding, 1798. Attempts have been made to introduce this species into Puget Sound, the results are unknown at this time.

Plate 29

187

188

189

188. *Ostrea lurida* Carpenter, 1864. The **Native** or **Olympia Oyster** is famous to gastronomes around the world. Found intertidally attached to rocks, and in commercial "farms" from northern British Columbia to Baja California.

189. *Crassostrea gigas* (Thunberg, 1793) is known also as the **Pacific** or **Japanese Oyster**. Introduced to many areas from its original Japanese waters it is now a very important commercial mollusk, millions of pounds being harvested each year. The illustration is 1/2 natural size.

PLATE 30

190. *Pseudochama exogyra* (Conrad, 1837) lives firmly attached to rocks and piling from the intertidal zone to depths of 60 feet, from central Oregon to Mexico and also in the Queen Charlotte Islands. Note the spiralling of the upper valve goes in the opposite direction to that of the next species. Common.

191. *Chama pellucida* Broderip, 1835. The **Jewel Box** occurs from central Oregon to southern Baja California in the inter and subtidal regions attached to rocks, piling and other objects. Note the numerous small spines and the spiralling which is counter-clockwise. Common in bays along the coast.

192. *Lucinoma annulata* (Reeve, 1850) is also called the **Ringed Lucine** and is uncommon in its range of northern British Columbia to southern California. Living from the intertidal to depths of 1,000 feet it can be distinguished by the "rings" of sculpture.

PLATE 31

193. *Kellia laperousei* Deshayes, 1839 is not uncommon intertidally and to depths of 150 feet from Alaska to Mexico. Usually found inside dead clam shells or other protected holes or crevices.

Plate 30

190

192

191

194. *Kellia suborbicularis* (Montagu, 1804) is very similar to the last species and ranges in the intertidal from the Queen Charlotte Islands to Mexico. Not uncommon.

195. *Glans subquadrata* (Carpenter, 1864) (Synonym: *G. carpenteri* Lamy). This small species can be found attached to the undersides of rocks from the intertidal zone to depths of 15 feet from northern British Columbia to Baja California and it is not uncommon.

196. *Astarte alaskensis* Dall, 1903. Found in depths of 150 to 600 feet this uncommon species ranges from the Bering Sea to Puget Sound.

197. *Astarte compacta* Carpenter, 1864. Another of this uncommon group of bivalves, this one inhabits depths of 60 to 600 feet from southern Alaska to Puget Sound.

198. *Astarte arctica* Gray, 1824. Ranging from the Arctic Ocean to British Columbia in depths of 100 to 700 feet, this species also occurs in the Atlantic.

199. *Cardita ventricosa* Gould, 1850 is a triangular bivalve which ranges from southern Alaska to Baja California and is commonly found in depths of 60 to 600 feet.

200. *Clinocardium fucanum* (Dall, 1907) is an uncommon species inhabiting depths of 50 to 1,000 feet from the Bering Sea to central California.

201. *Clinocardium californiense* (Deshayes, 1841) ranges from the Arctic Ocean to San Diego and also in Japan. From the intertidal zone to several hundred feet in sand or sandy/mud bottoms.

202. *Clinocardium nuttallii* (Conrad, 1837) is common intertidally and to depths of about 30 feet through most of its range from Alaska to San Diego. Attains

a maximum size of nearly five inches.

203. *Clinocardium ciliatum* (Fabricius, 1780). Ranging from the Bering Sea to Puget Sound this uncommon species lives in depths of 180 to 600 feet.

PLATE 32

204. *Nemocardium centifilosum* (Carpenter, 1864) is one of the smallest of our cockle group, distinguished by the line of demarcation in its sculpture. Ranging from Alaska to Baja California it is not uncommon in depths of 50 to 550 feet.

205. *Mactra californica* Conrad, 1837. Sand areas from the intertidal to 100 feet and from the Queen Charlotte Islands to Panama are the places to search for this species which is not common in our region.

206. *Macoma planuiscula* Grant and Gale, 1931. Uncommon, occurs from the Aleutian Islands to British Columbia in the intertidal to 300 feet zone.

207. *Serripes groenlandicus* Bruguière, 1789 is probably the rarest of all the cockle group in our area and is only found occasionally from the subtidal to 600 feet. Ranging in the Pacific from the Arctic to Washington it also occurs in the Atlantic. A fragile shell with purplish-pink interior it is a collector's prize.

208. *Spisula falcata* (Gould, 1850). The **Surf Clam** inhabits sandy beaches from the intertidal area to depths of 15 feet and occurs from northern British Columbia to Baja California. Not common.

PLATE 33

209. *Macoma calcarea* (Gmelin, 1792) is small, uncommon and occurs in depths of 100 to 600 feet from the Bering Sea to central California. Uncommon.

Plate 31

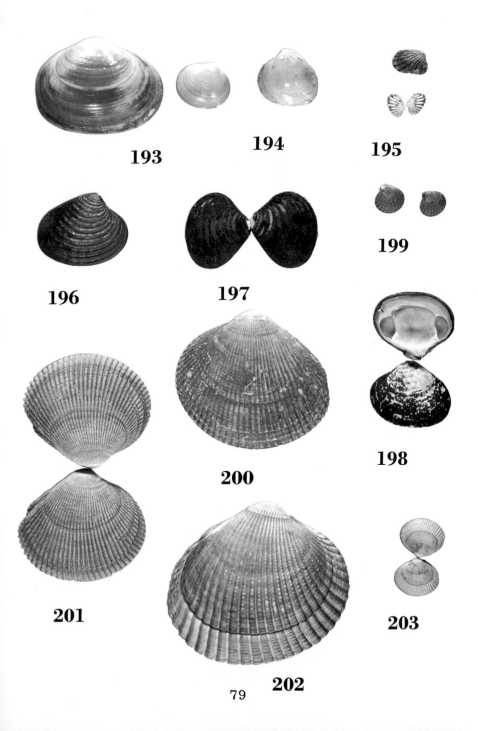

193

194

195

196

197

199

200

198

201

203

202

Plate 32

205

206

204

207

208

Plate 33

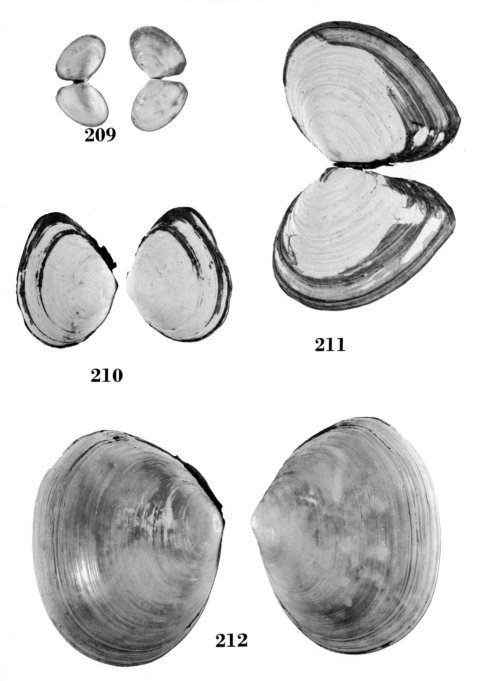

209

210

211

212

210. *Macoma irus* (Broderip and Sowerby, 1829) is a common intertidal resident of muddy sand flats from British Columbia to northern California.

211. *Macoma nasuta* (Conrad, 1837), the **Bent-Nose Clam** is a mud or sand dweller from the intertidal to 150 foot depths. Common, it ranges from Alaska to Baja California. There is a definite twist of the posterior end to the right when viewed from the umbo region.

212. *Macoma brota* Dall, 1916. An uncommon species inhabiting sand or mud bottoms in depths of 30 to 300 feet, this species occurs from Alaska to the Strait of Juan de Fuca.

PLATE 34

213. *Tellina bodegensis* Hinds, 1845 is uncommon, and a collector's prize throughout its range of northern British Columbia to Baja California on sand bars from the intertidal area to depths of 30 feet.

214. *Tellina carpenteri* Dall, 1900 is another prize to the shell collector who might find it anywhere in its range of northern British Columbia to Panama. Its habitat is the sand bottom from the intertidal to depths of 600 feet.

215. *Tellina buttoni* Dall, 1900 is probably the most common of the tellins in our region and can be found intertidally and to depths of 300 feet in sand from southern Alaska to Mexico.

216. *Tellina salmonea* (Carpenter, 1864) is uncommonly collected from southern Alaska to southern California and another species prized by the collector. It too lives in the sand from the intertidal to depths of 30 feet.

217. *Macoma inconspicua* (Broderip & Sowerby, 1829) is a common, sometimes highly colored little

Plate 34

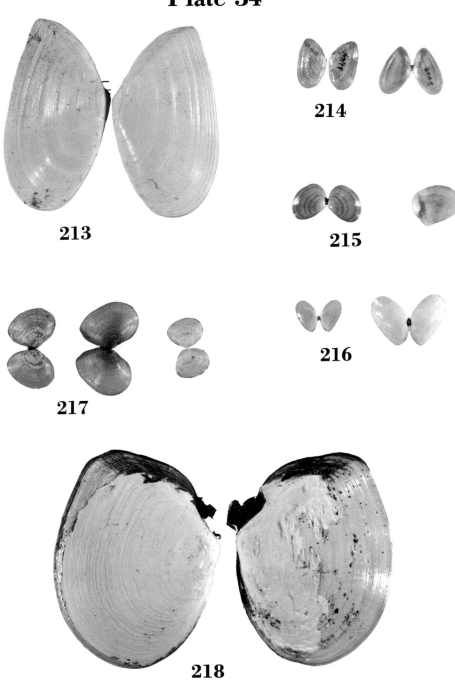

213

214

215

217

216

218

bivalve inhabiting muddy sand flats in the intertidal zone from the Bering Sea to southern California.

218. *Macoma secta* (Conrad, 1837), the **White Sand Clam**, is the largest species of this genus found anywhere and is common in sand or mud from southern Alaska to Mexico living from the intertidal zone to depths of 150 feet, The shell is somewhat chalky.

PLATE 35

219. *Tapes ?philippinarium* (Adams and Reeve, 1857), the **Manila Littleneck** is another of the accidental introductions to our region. It has become well established in many areas high in the intertidal, buried in sand and gravel. Note the elongate shape and yellowish interior. The animal has an orange tint. Very edible.

220. *Venerupis staminea* (Conrad, 1837), is the **Native Littleneck** which is quite common intertidally in sand and gravel from the Bering Sea to Mexico. A favorite when steamed and dipped in melted butter.

221. *Petricola carditoides* Conrad, 1837 lives in the intertidal zone in limestone rocks in empty pholad burrows. Ranging from Vancouver Island to San Diego this common bivalve varies greatly in shape because of the habitat in which it lives.

222. *Callithaca tenerrima* (Carpenter, 1857). The **Thin-Shelled Littleneck** is sometimes encountered in the gravel beach of the intertidal zone. Occuring from Vancouver Island to southern California this can be distinguished by its somewhat wedge-shape, cancellate sculpture, thin shell and large size.

223. *Entodesma saxicola* Baird, 1863, is the **Northern Ugly Clam** and can be found intertidally and to 60 feet nestled in crevices or attached to the undersides of rocks. Ranging from southern Alaska to

Plate 35

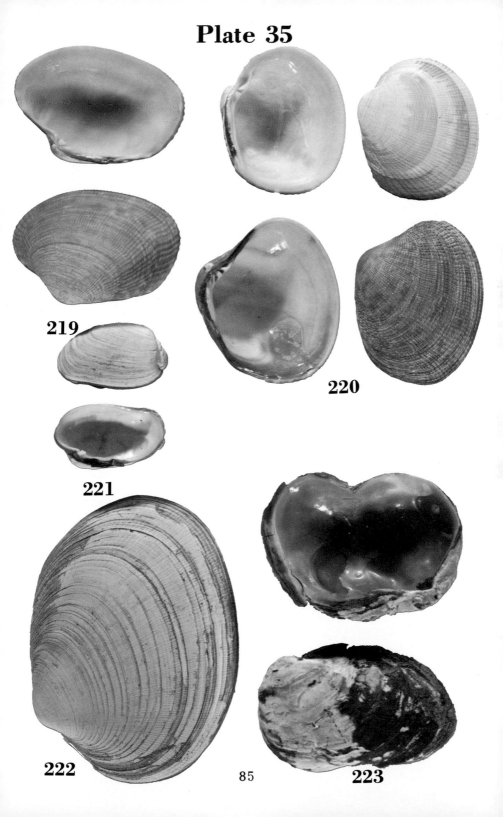

219

220

221

222

85

223

Plate 36

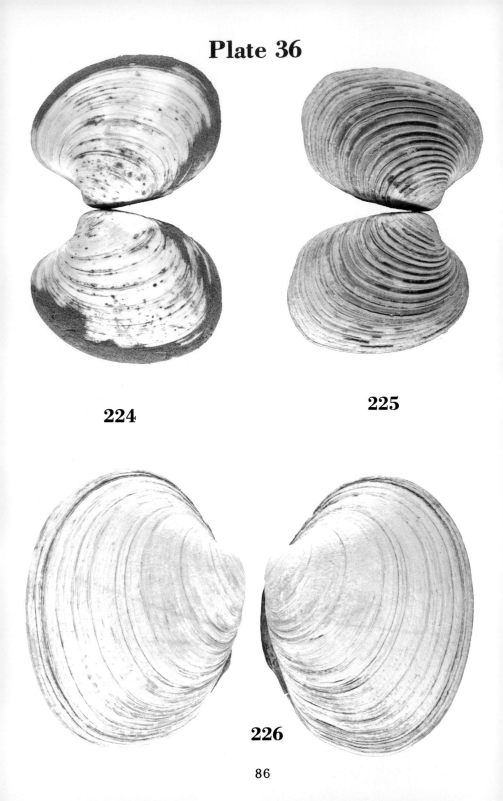

224

225

226

Baja California it is best to soak this species in glycerin to prevent the shell from shattering as the periostracum dries and contracts. Not uncommon.

PLATE 36

224. *Compsomyax subdiaphana* Carpenter, 1864. An uncommon bivalve that has the odd habit of constructing a "nest" of agglutinated sand in which to live. The range is British Columbia to southern California.

225. *Humilaria kennerleyi* (Reeve, 1863). This uncommon species ranges from southern Alaska to southern California and is found in sand and gravel from the intertidal to 150 foot depth. Note the deeply incised sculpture.

226. *Saxidomus giganteus* Deshayes, 1839. The well-known **Butter Clam** is very common from Alaska to northern California in the intertidal and to depths of 60 feet where it lives in sand and gravel. Prized for food.

PLATE 37 -Specimens Illustrated 1/2 Natural Size

227. *Panope generosa* Gould, 1850. The famous **Geoduc** of the Puget Sound region, it ranges from southern Alaska to Mexico and is more common in the subtidal zone than intertidally. This is the largest burrowing clam in the world and five pound specimens are not too unusual.

228. *Modiolus rectus* (Gould, 1842) is also known as the **Horse Mussel** and lives (intertidally to 30 feet) in sand with the hairy end sticking just above the surface. Ranging from northern British Columbia to the Gulf of California, it is not common.

229. *Zirfaea pilsbryi* Lowe, 1931, one of several species commonly called **Piddocks**, ranges from Alaska to southern Baja California. Living intertidally this bores into limestone or hard clay and while common is seldom secured. They do make a tasty chowder when available.

230. *Tresus nuttalli* (Conrad, 1837). One of two (No. 231 is the other) local species referred to as **Horse Clams**, this one can be distinguished by its more elongate shell. Range is from Vancouver Island to Baja California.

231. *Tresus capax* (Gould, 1850) ranges from Alaska to southern California and is more common than the last. More rounded in shape this also lives in sand or mud in the intertidal zone. One easy way to tell if the bivalve whose siphons you see sticking up from the sand is a horse clam or geoduc is to check that siphon closely, the geoduc's is always very clean while the horse clam's possesses auxiliary flaps of a horny material to which barnacles, algae and other items will attach.

PLATE 38

232. *Mya truncata* (Linné, 1758) is an uncommon bivalve inhabiting sand or mud bottoms in depths of 30 to 150 feet from the Bering Sea to Puget Sound. At first glance it looks like a small geoduc, but the hinge is a spoon-and-socket affair which is quite distinctive.

233. *Mya arenaria* (Linné, 1758), the **Eastern Soft-Shell Clam** is possibly an accidental introduction from the western Atlantic. It has become established on upper intertidal muddy beaches from northern British Columbia to central California and is common in some areas. A good food clam, this also has the odd spoon-and-socket hinge of No. 232.

Plate 37

227

228

229

230

231

Plate 38

232

233

234

235

90

234. *Siliqua patula* (Dixon, 1788). Next to the oyster the **Razor Clam** is probably our most valuable commercial bivalve. Found from the intertidal zone to depths of 120 feet it is common from Alaska to central California on hardpacked sand beaches.

235. *Solen sicarius* Gould, 1850. Locally common, the **Jacknife Clam**, is sometimes mistaken for the razor clam, but its slender shape and the hinge located close to one end distinguish it. Ranging from the Queen Charlotte Islands to Baja California it is found in sand in quieter waters than the above species which prefers the open coast sand beach.

PLATE 39

236. *Pandora filosa* (Carpenter, 1864). Found in depths of 40 to 600 feet on sand bottom from Alaska to southern California. Common.

237. *Pandora bilirata* Conrad, 1855 ranges from Alaska to Mexico and is not common on sand or mud bottoms in depths of 150 to 600 feet. Note that both valves of the *Pandora* group are concave.

238. *Pandora grandis* Dall, 1877, is a rare species taken in depths of 300 to 1,200 feet from Alaska to Oregon.

239. *Lyonsia californica* Conrad, 1837 is a small fragile species which occurs intertidally on sand flats amongst eel grass and to depths of 300 feet. The range is southern Alaska to Mexico and it is not common.

240. *Cardiomya pectinata* (Carpenter, 1864) is one of the oddly shaped bivalves known as spoon clams. This species is uncommon in depths of 30 to 500 feet from southern Alaska to Mexico.

241. *Netastoma japonica* (Yokoyama, 1920) is a rare species occasionally collected in British Columbia where it has been found intertidally boring in wood.

242. *Penitella penita* (Conrad, 1837) is a common **Piddock** which ranges from northern British Columbia to Baja California. It lives intertidally and to 15 feet boring into limestone.

243. *Zirfaea gabbi* Tryon, 1863 lives in the intertidal zone where it can be collected boring in limestone from southern Alaska to Baja California.

244. *Hiatella pholadis* (Linné, 1767) lives in kelp holdfasts and abandoned pholad burrows from the Bering Sea to southern California. Common.

245. *Hiatella arctica* (Linné, 1767). Quite common from the Bering Sea to Panama, this species is collected from the intertidal zone to depths of 300 feet attached to rocks, wood, etc. Also found in the Atlantic.

246. *Psephidia lordi* (Baird, 1863). Found from the intertidal (amongst eel grass roots) to depths of 300 feet on sand, this small species ranges from southern Alaska to central California. Common.

247. *Transenella tantilla* (Gould, 1853) is another small species, with a purplish blotch on one side. It too is found intertidally amongst the roots of eel grass and to a depth of 100 feet. The range is Vancouver Island to Mexico; common.

248. *Semele rubropicta* Dall, 1871. This colorful shell ranges from southern Alaska to Baja California. Uncommon, it can be found in gravel amongst rocks from the intertidal to depths of 60 feet.

249. *Gari californica* (Conrad, 1849) is another pink rayed clam which lives in sand from the intertidal to a depth of 30 feet. The range is southern Alaska to Baja California. Uncommon.

Plate 39

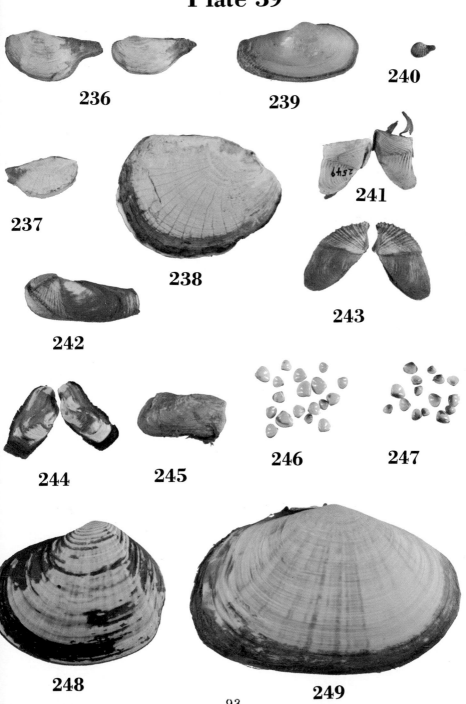

236

239

240

237

238

241

243

242

244

245

246

247

248

249

PLATE 40 - THE BRACHIOPODS

While not true mollusks these are included here as the shell collector will likely run across at least one species and need some assistance in identification. Differences between these and true bivalves are that these have an upper and lower (rather than right and left) valve; these have an organ, called a peduncle, for attachment to rocks, etc.; and these have an internal lyre-shaped "skeleton"; also, the brachiopod shell is not composed of calcium carbonate as are those of the true mollusks.

250. *Freilia halli* Dall, 1895. This transparent brachiopod lives in depths greater than 4,000 feet (the specimens illustrated came from over one mile deep!) and are extremely fragile. The range is the Bering Sea to San Diego, also Japan.

251. *Laqueus californicus* Koch, 1847. Ranging from British Columbia to southern California this smooth-shelled form is found in depths of 100 to 1,000 feet.

252. *Terebratalina unguicula* Carpenter, 1865, the **Snake's Head Lamp Shell** is found in depths of 100 to 1,000 feet from Kodiak Island, Alaska to Baja California.

253. *Terebratalia transversa caurina* (Gould, 1850). Found intertidally and to depths of 100 feet, this form of the following species ranges from Alaska to Puget Sound.

254. *Terebratalia transversa* (Sowerby, 1846). Found intertidally attached to stones near the low tide mark, and to depths of 500 feet, this smooth form ranges from Kodiak Island, Alaska to San Diego. Lines of growth are the only sculpture. The color when collected is brown, these specimens have had the outer periostracum removed to show the shell colors.

Plate 40

250

251

253

252

254

Books to Consult for Further Information

ABBOTT, R. TUCKER. 1954. *American Seashells*, D. Van Nostrand, Princeton, N.J.
" 1968. *Seashells of North America*, Golden Press, N. Y.
GRIFFITH, LELA M. 1967. *The Intertidal Univalves of British Columbia*, Handbook #26, British Columbia Provincial Museum.
HANNA, G. DALLAS. 1966. *Introduced Mollusks of Western North America*, California Academy of Sciences.
KEEN, A. MYRA. 1963. *Marine Molluscan Genera of Western North America: An Illustrated Key*, Stanford University Press.
McLEAN, JAMES H. 1969. *Marine Shells of Southern California*, Los Angeles County Museum of Natural History.
MORRIS, PERCY A. 1966. *A Field Guide to Shells of the Pacific Coast and Hawaii*, 2nd Edition. Houghton Mifflin, Boston.
OLDROYD, IDA S. 1924 *Marine Shells of the Puget Sound Region*, University of Washington Press.
QUAYLE, D. B. 1960. *The Intertidal Bivalves of British Columbia*, Handbook #17, British Columbia Provincial Museum.
RICE, THOMAS C. 1968. *A Checklist of the Marine Gastropods from the Puget Sound Region*, Of Sea & Shore Publications, Port Gamble, Washington.

OTHER PUBLICATIONS

OF SEA AND SHORE MAGAZINE. A quarterly devoted to the exploration of the animals and plants of the sea, lake, river and their shores with special emphasis on the shell life of these areas. P.O. Box 33; Port Gamble, Washington 98364. $3.50 per year (Quarterly); $1 per copy.

Index

The Index is arranged alphabetically and with *Italics* indicating
Plate Number and Species Number. Page Number of descriptions
are shown in regular type.

Glossary of Terms

aperture - the opening in a gastropod shell
apex - the point or tip of snail shells

base - the extremity opposite the apex; the bottom or lower part
byssus - silky threads secreted by bivalves to attach themselves to rocks

cancellate - latticed, cross-barred
columella - the central pillar of the snail shell around which the whorls are built

girdle - the part of the chiton holding the valves together

hinge - the portion of attachment of the two valves of Pelecypoda (clams)
holdfasts - portion of kelp which attaches the plant to the bottom

incised - sculptured with sharp, deep grooves
intertidal - the area bounded by the high and low tide

operculum - a horny or shelly plate which wholly or partially closes the aperture of a snail when the animal retracts

periostracum - a skin or horny covering on the exterior of many shells
punctate - covered or studded with dots

radiating - ribs extending from the center like rays
revolving - moving in a circular course; spiralling
ribs - long, narrow ridges

sculpture - the markings on a shells' surface; incised lines, depressed areas, ridges, etc.
shoulder - ridged, as in whorls of some gastropods, see figure just before explanation of Plate 6.
subtidal - living below the low tide area of the beach

umbilicus - an indentation, or depression, on the base of snail shells

whorls - one complete spiral turn of the spire of a snail

Pacific Northwest Shell Club, Inc. c/o 2237 N.E. 175th, Seattle, Wa. 98155.

Oregon Society of Conchologists; P.O. Box 3464, Portland, Oregon 97208.

Chico Shell Hounds; c/o Route 2, Box 79, Chico, California 95926.

Northern California Shell Club; c/o Steinhart Aquarium; California Academy of Sciences, San Francisco, California 94118.